THE 1926 GENERAL
WOLVERHAMPTON AND THE

THE 1926 GENERAL STRIKE IN WOLVERHAMPTON AND THE BLACK COUNTRY

A REVOLUTION OR A DISPUTE?

DAVID TAYLOR

YOUCAXTON PUBLICATIONS
OXFORD & SHREWSBURY

Copyright © David Taylor 2017

The Author asserts the moral right to
be identified as the author of this work.

ISBN 978-1-911175-99-5
Printed and bound in Great Britain.
Published by YouCaxton Publications 2017

All rights reserved. No part of this publication may be reproduced,
stored in a retrieval system, or transmitted in any form or by
any means, electronic, mechanical, photocopying, recording or
otherwise, without the prior permission of the publisher.

This book is sold subject to the condition that it shall not, by way of
trade or otherwise, be lent, resold, hired out or otherwise circulated
without the publisher's prior consent in any form of binding or cover
other than that in which it is published and without a similar condition
including this condition being imposed on the subsequent purchaser.

YouCaxton Publications
enquiries@youcaxton.co.uk

Contents

Introduction	ix
The Calling Of The General Strike	1
Government Preparations	7
Union Preparations	15
How Effective Were The Strikes?	24
How Loyal Were The Men To The Unions?	32
The Role Of Public Meetings	41
The Supply Of Fuel and Food	50
Reporting The General Strike	57
Photographs	61
The Churches	67
The Poor Law Unions And Unemployment Benefit (the dole)	71
Policing And The Courts	77
The End Of The General Strike	84
The Aftermath For The Unions	93
The Aftermath For Others	96
Was It An Industrial Dispute?	98
Or The Start Of A Revolution?	102
Conclusion	106
Appendix 1	
The Midland District Government Emergency Committee Officers	109
Biographical Notes	111
Bibliography	120
Index	125

My thanks to the Express and Star, Wolverhampton, and the Wolverhampton Civic and Historical Society who provided financial support through the Wolverhampton Archives History Symposium. In addition, the staff at the Express and Star kindly advised on the use of images and gave permission to use images from issues published at the time of the Strike. I am also grateful for the help of staff at the archive services of Wolverhampton, Dudley, Sandwell, Warwick Modern Records Centre and the National Archives in Kew. Last but not least, this book would not have taken shape without my wife, Alison, who proof-read the whole thing and listened to me talking about it for months.

Introduction

For nine days in May 1926 Britain was involved in a unique and variably interpreted conflict, a General Strike. Some perceived it to be the outcome of an impasse between the miners and the mine owners. For others, the union leadership was trapped into supporting the miners. Some saw it as an action forced on the trade unions as an inevitable consequence of the government's macro-economic strategy. For Marxists and Communists it was the opening salvoes of a revolution, started by 'capital's' assault on the 'workers'' living standards. For those on the radical left, it was an opportunity to implement a major change to the political process in support of the working class. For those on the right, it was inspired by the Soviet Union and aimed at unconstitutional government change. Still others saw it as the long awaited and carefully prepared for opportunity to reduce the power of the trade unions following a series of disputes showing their formidable power in the country.

In the Black Country these differences of opinion on the General Strike have been muted by the perception of it as a region dominated by right-wing trade unions, with a workforce in new industries immune to the radical calls of the left-wing of the trade unions or the Labour Party.[1] Certainly, in comparison to other areas, such as the North of England, South Wales and Glasgow, less appeared to happen. Even at the time, the region appeared to be overlooked. When the

---

1 Mary Davis, *Comrade Or Brother?: A History of the British Labour Movement 1789-1951* (London: Pluto Press, 1993), p. 132.

T.U.C. General Council sent Harold Croft on a tour of the country on 7th May to determine the effectiveness of the strike, he passed from Birmingham to the Potteries without mentioning the Black Country.² Ellen Wilkinson, the Marxist leaning Labour MP for Middlesbrough East, did not originally plan to visit Wolverhampton on her speaking tour and only attended because the local people 'demanded a meeting'.³ But strong emotions ran through the region. When Alfred Short, Labour MP for Wednesbury, spoke at the Great Bridge Market Place meeting on 9th May, he took as his theme the 'righteousness' of their cause.⁴ Some, especially those in the trade unions or on the radical end of the political spectrum, have noted the widespread reporting of strike activity across the region as indicative of the support for the strike by many of the communities of the Black Country.⁵

These contrasting opinions of the General Strike in the Black Country have rarely been examined. There have been very few articles and books on the subject. The Black Country trade union movement produced some pieces, mostly following the strike in 1926 and then again at the fiftieth anniversary in 1976. Historians have tended to look at either wider political issues, mainly based in London around the T.U.C. and the government, or they have investigated those areas with more dramatic events, such as the riots in Glasgow, or looked at specific issues across the country,

---

2 Croft, Harold, *Descriptive Account Of A Tour During The General Strike 1926*, Warwick, Modern Records Centre, MSS.292/252.62/13/25.

3 Lansbury's *Labour Weekly*, 22 May 1926.

4 *Dudley Herald*, 15 May 1926.

5 Speaker notes, Corbett, J., *Birmingham Trades Council, 1866-1966, Lawrence Wishart, 1966*, Warwick, Modern Records Centre, MSS.202B/S/12.

such as the role of women or the development of a civil protection programme.[6]

The most substantial work on the General Strike in the Black Country is George Barnsby's, based primarily on local press cuttings, the report of the Wolverhampton Trades and Labour Council Strike Committee to the T.U.C. after the strike, and various speakers' reports. His work gives a good overview of the majority of the material that is available. However, the purposes of this present work are, firstly, to more explicitly place the Black Country experience into a wider context, highlighting the similarities and differences to other areas. Secondly, it will investigate the material which has become available since the 1970s which adds to the 'colouring' of the event. However, it should be noted that some material is now deposited in archives which promise a lot but deliver very little about what happened. For example, the West Wolverhampton Labour Party minutes for 1926 do not mention the strike at all and there are only a few references to the continuing miners' strike.[7] Similarly, the Wolverhampton Number 6 Branch of the NUR makes no meaningful reference to the strike, despite meeting in the North Road Club, the headquarters for the NUR strike.[8] Thirdly, this

---

[6] See for example, Robert S Sephton, *Oxford And The General Strike 1926* (Oxford: Self Published, 1993). Anthony Mason, *The General Strike In The North East* (Hull: University Of Hull, 1970). Mary Davis, *"Comrade Or Brother?: A History of the British Labour Movement 1789-1951*, (London: Pluto Press, 1993). William Kenefick, 'The Fall of the Radical Left, c. 1920 to 1932', in *Red Scotland! The Rise and Fall of the Radical Left: c. 1872 to 1932*, ed. William Kenefick (Edinburgh: Edinburgh University Press, 2007). John McIlroy, Alan Campbell, Keith Gildart, *Industrial Politics and the 1926 Mining Lockout: The Struggle for Dignity* (Cardiff, University Of Wales Press, 2004).

[7] *Labour Party Minutes*, Wolverhampton, Archive, D/LAB/1/4.

[8] *NUR Wolverhampton Number 6 Branch Minute Book*, Wolverhampton, Archive, D/LAB/1/13.

work will widen the area examined as far as possible, from Wolverhampton to the whole of the Black Country. Of course, the perennial questions always arise of where is the Black Country and should Birmingham be included? The simple answer to the first question is 'as far as possible without straining the bounds of credibility'. For the second, 'Birmingham is not included because otherwise the balance would move substantially away from Wolverhampton, Walsall, Dudley and other towns in the area'. Finally, with the passing of the years, some of what was common knowledge will inevitably be lost, for example who people were and what they did. This work aims to gather at least some of this background knowledge into one place.

A point on sources needs to be made, that they are all subject to bias. This is particularly important to remember when considering that much of the information is gathered from local newspapers, which by and large were hostile to the trade union movement and to the calling of a strike over the condition of the mining industry, whether it was limited to miners or was made 'general'. Where appropriate this is specifically noted in the text, but it should be a background consideration throughout this work.

The Calling Of The General Strike

A series of different issues came together at the end of April 1926 which culminated in the calling of the General Strike by the General Executive of the T.U.C. The major issues were the economic condition of the mining industry, concerns regarding the influence of the Soviet Union and the Communist Party of Great Britain on British trade unions and the government's macro-economic strategy. These all played out against the disruption caused by World War One and its aftermath, including the Russian Revolution and the various peace treaties that concluded the war.

A series of mining disputes arose after World War One, centred on wages and hours, but involving other issues as well, such as the call from some on the far left for nationalisation. The immediate cause of the General Strike arose on 30th June, 1925 when the Mining Association, the representative body of the mine owners, gave notice that they would end the 1924 wage agreement, allowing them to cut wages and increase hours. In the following negotiations it was apparent that, without a subsidy, a strike or lock-out was inevitable. The government reviewed its emergency arrangements and Stanley Baldwin, the prime minister, concluded that they 'were not ready'. Therefore, the government backed down, provided a subsidy for the coal industry to last nine months to enable the employers to maintain wages and conditions, and set up another Royal Commission.[9] This occurred on 31st July 1925 and became known as Red Friday. In September 1925 parliament approved the subsidy until 30th

---

[9] Patrick Renshaw, *The General Strike* (London: Eyre Methuen, 1975), pp 117-118.

April, 1926[10]. At a cost of approximately £750,000 a week, it was a substantial outgoing for the government at a time when they wanted to balance their income and expenditure. The subsidy drew accusations of profiteering on the mine owners. Certainly it was a substantial subsidy for the mine owners without apparent strings. For the Earl of Dudley's Baggeridge and Himley collieries, it amounted to £31,287 for the nine months, which appeared to be about 25% of the cost of wages and more than doubled their profitability.[11]

The Samuel Royal Commission investigated what could and should be done about the industry. It found that many mines, 47% in Eastern England and 100% in Northumberland, ran at a loss and that as much as 73% of coal produced in the last quarter of 1925 was produced at a loss before the subsidy.[12] It found that many of the mines in Brierley Hill were 'broken', unable to operate without financial assistance. The commission's recommendations, published on 10th March, 1926, were for reorganisation to put the coal mining industry on to an economic basis, hopefully without mass redundancies. The miners would have to accept a temporary reduction in wages and an increase in hours, reversing the increases in wage rates that had occurred during the First World War and the immediate post-war years.[13] The aim was to spread the cost across the country. If not, there would be substantial bankruptcies and redundancies focused

---

10 Viscount Samuel, *Memoirs* (London, The Cresset Press, 1945), p 183.

11 Re-worked figures from the *Earl Of Dudley's Baggeridge Colliery Ltd Half Year Report 1926*, Dudley, Archive, DE/7/2/2/3.

12 Samuel, *Memoirs*, p 185.

13 The Earl of Dudley's Baggeridge and Himley collieries reported average sales price reductions of 3.6% and 11.9% respectively for the first four months of 1926 compared to 1925. Re-worked figures from the *Earl Of Dudley's Baggeridge Colliery Ltd Half Year Report 1926*, Dudley, Archive, DE/7/2/2/3.

in specific areas.[14] The government accepted the report in its entirety with some minor disagreements; the mine owners were prepared to go along with the report; but the Miners' Federation were opposed to any reduction in wages or increase in hours. 'Not a minute on the day, not a penny off the pay' was their slogan. Negotiations began, but it became clear to the mine owners that the unions would not move on their position. So on 15th April they gave notice that the existing rates of pay would be ended on 30th April, the same day as the subsidy ended. New rates would be applied from 1st May.[15]

Many in the government and on the right wing of British politics perceived that there was a longstanding threat to the British constitution.[16] This came from two different but connected sources. Firstly, there was the power of trade unionism and an associated socialist ideology. Secondly there was the influence of the Soviet Union through the Communist Party of Great Britain. The perceived threat from trade unionism and socialism went back to before the First World War, but gathered importance after 1918. In 1924, the General Council of the T.U.C. was established, with an objective, amongst others, of promoting 'common action by the trade union movement'. Part of Baldwin's campaign in the December 1924 general election was based on the dangers of socialism. This threat was then further crystallised in 1925 around the events of Red Friday, as previously outlined.

At the same time, there was a background of concern regarding the involvement of the Soviet Union in British politics and industrial relations. The Zinoviev letter of 1924, although

---

14 Samuel, *Memoirs*, p 186.

15 Samuel, *Memoirs*, p 186.

16 Kevin Quinlan, *The Secret War Between the Wars: MI5 in the 1920s and 1930s* (Woodbridge, Suffolk: Boydell Press, 2014), pp 37-39.

undoubtedly a forgery, raised the spectre of the Soviet Union funding activities by the Communist Party of Great Britain calling for the mobilisation of labour against the government. This fuelled a perception of an organised attempt to undermine the constitution of Britain by British and overseas communist groups.[17] There were reports that the Communist Party of Great Britain, as directed by the Soviet Union, intended to use the General Council as a way of directing the T.U.C. and the whole Trade Union movement. This appeared to be confirmed by the founding and apparently rapid development of the National Minority Movement, as a link between the Communist Party of Great Britain and the trade unions. This contributed to the government's decision to provide the funding to the mining industry in July 1925. Therefore, in April 1926, Baldwin saw the call for a General Strike more as a threat to the basic tenets of law and order, 'nearer to proclaiming a civil war than we have been for centuries past', than as an industrial issue.[18]

The government itself contributed to the widespread labour problems with its macro-economic strategy. Along with industrial and social aspects of the Conservative Party policy of 1924 was an economic policy based on a desire to return to pre-1914 conditions as quickly as possible. This centred on re-establishing free trade, reducing government debt and returning to the pre-1914 gold standard. This policy implied deflation in the economy along with a reduction in wage levels. It also required that unemployment would not be a top concern for the government. However, conditions in Britain had been changed by the First World War. There had been wage inflation, especially

---

17 Quinlan, p 43.

18 Quinlan, p 32.

in industries which had benefited from wartime demand, such as engineering, mining, chemicals, steel, and shipbuilding. Further, with the relative shortage of manpower, especially towards the end of the war, there had been an increase in trade union power. Therefore, the macro-economic policy was amended in practice with, for example, empire preference easing out free trade, more consideration given to levels of unemployment due to the fear of the unrest it would create, and allowing the continuation of cartels and monopolies set up to increase efficiency during the war. Unfortunately, the benefits of the pre-1914 gold standard were perceived to be high, in effect giving Britain an opportunity to regain or even advance its world pre-eminence in finance and trade.[19] Therefore, this aspect of its macro-economic policy was pursued despite its incongruence with economic conditions at the time. In April 1925, the British government passed the Gold Standard Act. Almost immediately the effects and the reactions were felt in the economy.

The establishment of the pre-1914 gold standard, with an implied reduction in wages; the ending of the mining subsidy without agreement between the miners' union, the mine owners and the government; the greater emphasis within the trade union movement for concerted action; and the fear of external and internal challenges to the British constitution were all focused into two weeks at the end of April 1926. Not until then, as the situation was approaching a crisis,[20] did the government enter into active negotiations with both sides. Unfortunately, on Friday, 30th April, negotiations between the miners' union and the mine owners broke down, and the subsidy to the mines

---

19 John McIlroy, et al, pp 20-23.

20 Bernard Wasserstein, *Herbert Samuel: A Political Life* (Oxford, Clarendon Press, 1992), p 282.

ceased. A state of national emergency was declared by the king at Buckingham Palace and distributed to the provinces by telegram at 11:30am. On Saturday, 1st May the mine owners posted at the pits the previously announced new terms of employment. The coal miners rejected them and went on national strike. The government activated its preparations for the General Strike. Most of these preparations had been in secret and had not been fully tested. Even the names of those on the different Government Emergency Committees were not widely distributed. On the same day, the T.U.C. called a General Strike to begin at one minute to midnight on Monday, 3rd May. During Sunday, 2nd May there were continuous negotiations between the T.U.C., now acting on behalf of the Miners' Federation, and the government. Late in the day, the printers at the Daily Mail refused to print the London edition because of an editorial highly critical of the General Strike. Baldwin ended negotiations, on the basis that he would not negotiate whilst the freedom of the press was threatened. The General Strike was going ahead and formally started late on Monday night.

Government Preparations

The key legislation for the government's preparations was the Emergency Powers Act of 1920. This was passed after industrial action in 1919 and 1920, particularly in the mines and on the railways, showed that strikes in certain industries could have a substantial impact on the nation as a whole. This legislation allowed the king to proclaim a state of emergency if there was a threat of, or actual, activities which would 'extensively interfere with the supply and distribution of food, water, fuel or light, or the means of locomotion [which would] deprive a substantial proportion of the community with the essentials of life'. This proclamation gave the government powers to take any action essential to the public safety and the life of the community. There were only two exceptions: the government could not impose compulsory military service, and no regulation could be passed to make it an offence to take part in a strike or to peacefully persuade others to take part. Other legal and regulatory arrangements were also put into place, for example to allow the impounding of wirelesses to aid rapid communication.

As part of the fear of the external threat to the British constitution, the government decided to reduce the effectiveness of the Communist Party of Great Britain. It was never a large body of people. In 1925 it had 5,000 members, which peaked at 11,500 by the end of 1926, but by 1928 it was back down to 5,000.[21] However, for the government it appeared to be able to wield greater influence than its numbers implied, due to its

---

21 John McIlroy et al, p 271-272.

connections to the Soviet Union, its organisation and focus on a single goal, supposedly the overthrow of the British constitution, and its close connections to the trade union movement. In August 1925, seven of its national committee members were imprisoned for terms of up to a year for inciting mutiny, by encouraging soldiers not to obey orders. At the same time their offices were closed down, their equipment seized, and they were generally placed on close surveillance.[22]

The government established the Organisation For The Maintenance of Supplies (O.M.S.) to provide support in an emergency, by gathering the details of people who would make themselves available to assist the government and implement its emergency plans. By mid-1926, it was reported to have 75,000 members nationally. Finally, the government changed its contingency plans from small scale and theoretical into large scale and practical. Overall control and administration during the emergency was to be managed through the Ministry of Health. England and Wales were divided into ten districts, whilst Scotland was treated as one district, each controlled by a commissioner given widespread powers to deal with transport, food, postal services and fuel.[23] The Black Country was part of the Midland District, which covered the counties of Staffordshire, Shropshire, Worcestershire, Warwickshire and Herefordshire. Their Commissioner was Lieutenant-Colonel Hon George Frederick Stanley, MP for Willesden East.[24] Their offices were Newspaper House, 174 Corporation Street, Birmingham.

---

22 Quinlan, p.50.

23 Julian Symons, *The General Strike : a historical portrait* (London, Cresset Press, 1957), p.25.

24 See Appendix 1 for a schedule of his assistants.

For the Black Country two further Government Emergency Committees were established: one to cover Wolverhampton, Dudley, Stourbridge and the immediate surrounding districts, with its headquarters in Wolverhampton; the other in Walsall, consisting of Walsall Borough, Darlaston U.D.C. and Walsall R.D.C.. Below these, the government's organisation was based on local government authorities. Sub-committees were set up in each town or district. No matter what level it was in the hierarchy, each Government Emergency Committee had a Food Officer, a Road Officer, a Haulage Committee and a Coal Emergency Officer. Other representatives were recruited as required by the local conditions. The roles and responsibilities of each officer were broadly defined to plan and coordinate their areas of responsibility. For example, the Food Officer was to liaise with local traders to determine stocks and establish rationing as required, maintaining the distribution of food through normal channels. The Road Officer was to prioritise and economise the use of vehicles for road haulage, whilst the Coal Emergency Officer was to plan and coordinate the supply and distribution of coal, including any rationing required in their district. They were to issue permits and then liaise with area and district Emergency Committee Coal Officers to source the coal for these demands. Where demand could not be fulfilled the various Coal Officers had to determine how best to use the available coal.[25]

In addition to the Government Emergency Committees, there were three other strands to the government's preparations. A network of government-appointed chairmen was established to convene and oversee a Volunteer Service Committee, specifically

---

[25] For an example of how the system was perceived in practice see the *Earl Of Dudley's Baggeridge Colliery Ltd Half Year Report 1926*, Dudley, Archive, DE/7/2/2/3.

to recruit volunteers. The chief constables were, as normal, tasked to make arrangements for the enrolment of enough special constables as required to deal with the situation in their jurisdictions. The third strand was that local authorities were made responsible for maintaining local public utility services, and to assist in the maintenance of local transport and coal distribution. However, they were not to be involved in the distribution of food, nor for shipping, railway or postal communications, nor the docks and harbours unless they were the port authority.

By 22nd February, 1926, the Home Secretary, William Joynson-Hicks, reported to the cabinet that 'all that had to be done, was done', and now it only remained to wait for 'any emergency'.[26] In practice, whilst many of the arrangements were completed, not all of the councils and committees were ready at that point. Some councils had been late in reviewing the instructions that came from national government. West Bromwich borough council did not discuss the Ministry of Health Circular Letter no. 636, dated 20th November, 1925, which covered council responsibilities regarding 'Industrial disputes and the maintenance of Local Services', until their meeting on 6th January, 1926.[27] Other councils were late in setting up their committees. Kingswinford reported that their Government Emergency Committee had not completed its arrangements by 8th May, some of which, including that for coal deliveries, were not completed until 11th May, the day before the end of the General Strike.[28] It took until 10th May to appoint Bilston's Government Emergency Committee on food supplies.[29]

---

26 Quinlan, p.45.

27 *Minutes of West Bromwich Council Meetings, 6th January 1926,* Sandwell, Archive, CB-B/1/39.

28 *Express and Star,* 8 May 1926 and 11 May 1926.

29 *Express and Star,* 10 May 1926.

However, these delays in some local authority areas was not critical, as it turned out, because of the short duration of the General Strike.

Nearly everywhere the members of the local authorities, either as a group or as individuals, decided to fill the various roles on the Government Emergency Committees themselves. In West Bromwich borough, it consisted of the mayor, Thomas Cottrell; the Motor and Transport Committee Chairman, Alderman Turley; the Electricity Committee Chairman, Councillor Bell; the Gas Committee Chairman, Alderman Cox; the Finance Committee Chairman, Alderman Bache; and the Watch Committee Chairman, Councillor Lellow.[30] In Walsall, the committee was presided over by the mayor, councillor David Parry. In Wolverhampton and District, the chair was the mayor, Frederick Willcock. In Dudley, it was chaired by the mayor, T W Tanfield. In Darlaston, Councillor F C Wesson was elected as the chairman.

This overlap between local authority and Government Emergency Committee members was to have an effect on relationships and actions. The government seemed to assume that their Emergency Committees would work smoothly to break the strike, in effect, no matter what the councillors' political views might be. The portents were that it was unlikely to be that easy. At the Mayday demonstration of the West Bromwich Labour Party, Councillor Joe Bailey asked for the T.U.C. to call out all workers as soon as possible and the Right Honourable Frederick Roberts, MP for the borough, sent a telegram saying 'Regret cannot join in great adventure demonstration. Keep calm and united and victory assured.'[31]

---

30 *Minutes of West Bromwich Council Meetings, 5th May 1926,* Sandwell, Archive, CB-B/1/39:

31 *Dudley Herald,* 15 May 1926.

Perhaps the best reported difficulties occurred at Wolverhampton Town Council's meeting on Monday, 10th May, where there was a sizeable Labour minority.

Number of Councillors	Conservative	Liberal	Independent	Labour	Total
	21	11	3	13	48

Table from G. W. Jones, *Borough Politics : A Study of the Wolverhampton Town Council 1888-1964* (London, MacMillan and Co, 1969), p 360.

The problems started with the agenda. It had been printed and distributed some days previously, before the General Strike had been called, therefore it did not include a discussion of the General Strike. The Labour members of the council wanted to discuss the General Strike but the mayor said it was not on the agenda so it could not be discussed, except at the end of the meeting. There followed a convoluted set of proposals and discussions trying to allow the strike to be discussed in full within the main body of the meeting, all of which failed when voted on.

Then the question of who should be members of the Government Emergency Committee was raised. After a lively debate, seven members were chosen as a sub-committee of the General Purposes Committee. They were the mayor, Willcock, and aldermen Bantock, Evans, Myatt, Jeffs, Jenks, Lee and Mander, all of them either Conservative or Liberal Party representatives. During the debate, Alderman Bantock, Liberal, said that 'he will not serve on the committee with Labour members, the town had to be ruled by those who wanted to get the men back to work, not those who were wanting to move them away from work'.

There then followed a debate about approving the implementation of a plan for a bus service manned by volunteers. Clearly, as far as the Labour members were concerned, this was a 'strike breaking' activity using 'blacklegs' that they did not want implemented. They attempted both to defeat and then delay the decision, but in the end it was approved by 21 votes to 16. Finally, the Labour councillors were able to propose a resolution on the General Strike to be approved by the council. Again, after some debate and amendments, a resolution was agreed that 'Wolverhampton Town Council called for the government to resume negotiations on the basis of a return to the status quo, withdrawal of the General Strike and the mine owners' notices and the continuance of the subsidy for another month.'.[32]

At West Bromwich Council Meeting on the following day, several matters of a 'contentious character' due to the strike were withdrawn from the reports presented to the meeting. These included the proposal with regard to the salary of the Medical Officer of Health, the opening of the playing fields, and the report on the subject of birth control. What could be contentious in these is not clear, but obviously there was something, presumably between the different parties represented on the council. However, despite these precautions, Labour Party councillors brought up the subject of the General Strike. Councillor Wills complained that 'the Transport Committee had brought into operation black-leg labour to run buses into Birmingham'. Alderman Arnold, Conservative, said 'they had considered the girls who had to travel to and from Birmingham to work' when making the decision, whilst the mayor, Thomas Cottrell, remarked that 'with the committee he took full responsibility for the running of these buses. The committee were

---

[32] *Minutes Of Meeting Of Wolverhampton Council,* Wolverhampton, Archive, LS/L352.

determined that these buses should be run and to be perfectly frank he was in agreement with the committee.' It was also noted in the minutes that members of the public in the Public Gallery 'broke into applause when Councillor Wills spoke' and in response the Mayor warned them that 'at the next ebullition either he would vacate the chair or the applauders would be out'.[33]

These differences continued to surface in the months following the General Strike, whilst the miners continued their strike. In November the West Bromwich borough council voted on a proposal for the Government to 'take action at once to secure the immediate withdrawal of the Lock-out Notices in the Mining Industry and to carry out the re-organisation of that industry.' This was defeated by 23 votes to 8.[34] The split was almost entirely along party lines.[35]

At least in these council meetings the General Strike was discussed. At Walsall Council Meeting on Tuesday, 11th May there was a vote on whether a councillor should be heard at the end of the ordinary business of the council, unfortunately no subject is given in the newspaper, the assumption is that it was to do with the General Strike. The proposal was defeated.[36]

---

33 *'Strike Bulletin'*, No. 1 and 2, Sandwell, Archive, BS-KJ/8/3/5.

34 *Minutes of West Bromwich Council meetings (9 Nov 1925 - 8 Nov 1926)*, Sandwell, Archive, CB-B/1/39.

35 Those for were Bailey, Bellingham, Davies, Mynett, Poultney, Sutton, Wills and Wilson, mainly Labour supporters. Those against were Arnold, Bache, Bell, Cox, Kenrick, Lawley, Turley and Wheatley, Adams, G E Cottrell, Crump, Garratt, Gill, Grant, Hazel, Lellow, Mercer, Prince, Round, Smith, Spring, Willcock and Woodward, mainly Conservative or Liberal councillors.

36 *Express and Star*, 11 May 1926.

Union Preparations

In contrast to the government's efforts, the trade unions appeared to be very relaxed. Some people outside the General Council of the T.U.C. did make many suggestions that the trade unions had to be organised in advance to successfully implement a General Strike. George Lansbury, editor of the *Daily Herald*, the leading trade union supporting daily newspaper, suggested that the national network of Trades Councils should be used to draw together the local branches of all the main unions across the country, and that they be made the regional representatives of the General Council, allowing local decision making. He also suggested that food supplies should be managed through the Co-operative Societies, and that an unarmed Workers' Defence Corps should be set up to act as a police force on the side of the trade unions, in effect creating structures that could assist in the control of the country during the General Strike. But all these suggestions were ignored.[37] Instead there was to be a reliance on traditional trade union values and methods.

This was for a variety of reasons but mainly because, firstly, the T.U.C. leadership had changed, and new leaders in 1926 were less militant than those had been in 1925, and secondly, at a national level, the trade unions had conflicting objectives and approaches, each trade union wanting to maintain its independence, and the various leaders were wary of each other. To complicate matters further, some of the unions were themselves federations and thus the executives had to be very careful about what they agreed to or

---

37 Raymond Postgate, *The Life Of George Lansbury* (London, Longman, Green and Co, 1951), p 236.

committed their federation to do. For many, their rules explicitly forbade them from delegating powers to another body.[38] As well as hindering preparations, these factors affected the style of the preparations. In contrast to the government, the T.U.C. Strike Organisation Committee wanted to keep a tight centralised control of the General Strike, and all 'hour by hour' decisions were to be made by them.[39]

Not until the afternoon of Wednesday, 28th April did the arrangements begin to be made.[40] A Special Committee was appointed under the General Council of the T.U.C. to deal with matters as they arose. Each separate union involved was to have its own strike committee. The existing local Trades Councils were to act as local organising committees, coordinating the efforts of the different trade unions and other bodies to implement the strike. However, in most cases they had no paid officials and no premises of their own. They in turn set up with local trade unions, strike committees variously called Council of Action, Strike Committee or, confusingly, Emergency Committee. They were to handle publicity, transport permits, picketing, relief of distress, provision of food, entertainment and sport on behalf of the T.U.C.. In practice, these Councils of Action became pivotal in ensuring the effectiveness of the strike at the local level, coordinating local actions.[41]

In Wolverhampton, the Trades and Labour Council Executive Committee met specially on Monday, 3rd May to consider the 'coal

---

38 Margaret Morris, *The British General Strike 1926* (London, Journeyman Press, 1980), p 280.

39 Symons, p 137.

40 Hamilton Fyfe, *Behind The Scenes Of The Great Strike* (London, Whitefriars Press, 1926), 11th May.

41 Symons, pp 145 and 149.

crisis'. An Emergency Committee was appointed consisting of R. H. Allport as chairman, H. Barrett as secretary, Dan Davies and Councillor R. J. Evans as the legal advisor. They were given 'full powers to coordinate the unions involved'. Their first action was to create a further Emergency Committee with representatives from each of the unions affected in the first call for strike action, namely the Transport men, Typographical Association, NATSOPER, E.T.U., and some members of A.E.U. and Allied Trades and Building Trades Workers. However, their reports indicate that there were only six members on the Emergency Committee, so how it was constructed in practice is not clear.[42]

It first met on Tuesday, 4th May. Its first problem was 'interpreting the general circular sent by the T.U.C.' defining its role. The fact that there was confusion in its role definition highlighted very clearly the lack of preparation and the divisions within the various parts of the trade union movement. At first, the circular stated that they were to work with the 'trade unions actually participating in the dispute' to 'assist in carrying out' the 'stoppage of work in various trades and undertakings, and exception thereto'. However, the circular went on to say that they had the 'responsibility of organising the trade unionists in dispute in the most effective manner for the preservation of peace and order'.[43] Some members of the Emergency Committee thought they had 'the authority to call workers to cease work', whilst others thought that their role was to 'carry out the wishes of the General Council and to coordinate the calling out of the men from the

---

42 *Wolverhampton Trades and Labour Council Report*, Warwick, Modern Records Centre, MSS.292/252.62/5/52.

43 Burns, Emile, *The General Strike, May 1926: Trades Councils in action*' (London, The Labour Research Department, 1926), Warwick, Modern Records Centre MSS.15X/2/266/40, p 7.

different unions'. It would appear that this difference of opinion continued throughout the General Strike, because in the report after the strike Allport and Barrett stated that they, as authors of the report, 'agreed with this interpretation of their role'.[44]

The next set of problems again indicated a lack of preparation, 'waiting for instructions from the leadership of each of the unions to cease work' and reconciling and coordinating the different instructions the various unions sent to their branches. This was 'most evident in the Building Trades'. Some of the Builders' unions instructed their members to strike on any site except those for housing, hospital and sanitation. However, all building workers wanted to strike in support of the miners. On Saturday, 8th May, the local building workers asked their national unions, by telegram, for an instruction that all building workers should cease work. Meanwhile, the first instructions received concerning the Engineers were described as 'very vague and there was much discussion about whether they applied to the Motor Industry'. This problem was overcome when 'Vehicle Builders received specific instructions to strike'. These problems were presumably being experienced in other locations, because the General Council of the T.U.C. issued a general instruction that if any union executive called a strike, all other union men in a factory that was affected were also to cease work in that factory. This helped to resolve some of the disagreements about who was to strike in a specific location. It also provided a multiplicative effect to an individual union's calling of a strike. For example it was reported that 'very quickly there was a complete stoppage of the motor industry in Wolverhampton'. In Wolverhampton, the general situation was further complicated by the 'railway groups' setting up a separate

---

44 *Wolverhampton Trades and Labour Council Report*, Warwick, Modern Records Centre, MSS.292/252.62/5/52.

strike committee, which met on a daily basis at the North Road Club, called the North Road Joint Committee.[45]

'Communication and lack of reliable information' was seen as the next major problem to be tackled. Dan Davies was delegated to set up lines of communication from Wolverhampton to Birmingham and from there down to London; to the north through Stafford, Stone and Manchester; and to Chester and North Wales through Wellington and Shrewsbury. Due to a reluctance to use the usual lines of communication, which were thought to be susceptible to interception by government agencies, most of these arrangements were of 'volunteer despatch riders', mainly union volunteers who had access to a motorbike. The use of motorbikes for communication purposes spread to many different parts of the strike. The busmen's picket at the Midland Red garage in Dudley used 'motor cycling members [to] keep in touch with other districts'.[46] Motorbikes were used to transport speakers to venues, Jim Simmons recalls being 'precariously perched on the back of a motor-cycle – a gymnastic exercise which my artificial leg made a little difficult' as he 'careered around the district, addressing meetings of strikers and urging potential allies to join in the fray.'[47] To link the Black Country to the rest of the country, Dan Davies was appointed to 'act on behalf of the T.U.C. for all the towns between Dudley and Oswestry'. He was to receive a report each day from each strike committee, send out official information from the T.U.C., supply speakers

---

45 *Wolverhampton Trades and Labour Council Report*, Warwick, Modern Records Centre, MSS.292/252.62/5/52.

46 *Express and Star*, 7 May 1926.

47 Jim Simmons, *Soap-Box Evangelist*, (Chichester, Janay Publishing Company, 1972), pp 72-82.

and forward information to the General Council in London.[48] A huge responsibility given his available resources.

The Trade Councils' lack of resources is reflected in the bulletins they issued to communicate to the general public compared to the government's *British Gazette*, which approached 1,500,000 copies at its peak publication. The Wednesbury Trade Council issued two editions of its bulletin, one on each Sunday, 750 copies on the first and 1,000 copies on the second, whilst in Wolverhampton there was a daily edition of 500 copies from 5th May for six days.[49] It is also notable that the same names appeared throughout the strike, indicating a reliance on a small number of highly energetic people. At the start of the second week of the strike, it was reported in the *Express and Star* that Charles Sitch MP 'addressed over 40 meetings in the Black Country, over the last week'. This reliance on a narrow base of people to lead the local strike may account for the report that, in Wednesbury and Darlaston, the local Labour Party had ceased 'political activities' and formed 'strike Emergency Committees'.[50]

This lack of resources also reduced their effectiveness in pressing forward the T.U.C.'s programme of strikes. Even an energetic trades council such as Wolverhampton's had very limited effectiveness in many areas of the conflict. One of the roles of the Trades and Labour Council Emergency Committees was to 'assist in carrying out' the 'stoppage of work'. In this regard, they dealt with local authorities to add weight to the individual unions' actions. The Wolverhampton committee sent a 'deputation to the mayor and town clerk' regarding the actions of the police, led by the chief

---

48 *Wolverhampton Trades and Labour Council Report*, Warwick, Modern Records Centre, MSS.292/252.62/5/52.

49 Burns, appendix.

50 *Express and Star*, 7 May 1926.

constable, during an incident involving a private charabanc, which they noted was operating illegally. The mayor gave them 'very little satisfaction' for this and 'other serious complaints' regarding the actions of the special constables. It may be as a follow up action that the Trades and Labour Council Emergency Committee sent a letter to the Wolverhampton Borough Council on 25th May about the actions of the special constables. The council noted its receipt but the council minutes do not indicate any response.[51] A little after their visit to the mayor, the T.U.C. Special Committee sent a telegram to the Wolverhampton Emergency Committee asking them to come to an arrangement with the management of the Commercial Road power station so that it would only 'supply power to houses, street lighting, shops, social services, food production, bakers, domestic purposes and laundry'. The management refused the request so 'the T.U.C. sent instructions to remove all men from the power station'. This seemed to have very little impact on the operating of the station.[52]

Inevitably, workers in different areas progressed at different speeds in organising themselves. It was not until Thursday, 6th May that the miners from Cradley Heath formed a strike committee to cooperate with other committees in the affected trades of their area. Charles Sitch, a name that appears many times in the records, was noted as being in attendance and assisted in setting up this committee.[53]

With a lack of resources, and wireless communication unavailable to them, the strikers' main method of communicating with the

---

51 *Minutes Of Meeting Of Wolverhampton Council 14th June 1926*, Wolverhampton, Archive, LS/L352.

52 *Wolverhampton Trades and Labour Council Report*, Warwick, Modern Records Centre, MSS.292/252.62/5/52.

53 *Dudley Herald,* 8 May 1926.

general public, workers and trade union men was the public meeting. Over the weekend of 1st and 2nd May, a wide range of different meetings was held across the Black Country. Mostly, these had been previously organised as part of the May-day celebrations. Charles Sitch and A. Short, Labour MPs for Kingswinford and Wednesbury respectively, held a meeting at the Rowley Labour Club.[54] There was a series of meetings for the miners where they were told that all they had to do was to 'hold our nerve and stand firm' along with a general request 'to keep our heads and tempers'. In Wolverhampton, there was a parade through the town of tableaux and trade union banners, with speeches in the Market Square. Again Charles Sitch, along with Mrs Harrison Bell, the local Labour Party organiser, spoke to 500 people. Mrs Bell talked about the unfair distribution of wealth, coal royalties as a hidden tax on the people, and inefficiencies in the industry that could be corrected by nationalisation. She called for loyalty to the unions and the defeat of the blackleg organisation which the government was organising with tax payers' money. Both speakers asked that, if a general stoppage were called, the people should 'keep their tempers, give no cause for trouble but, above all, remain loyal to their unions.' This message of loyalty was included in the NUR instruction issued over the weekend, which finished with 'perfect loyalty will ensure success.'[55] On the Sunday evening, the Workers' Institute at Cradley Heath was described as 'packed' for the annual May Day rally of the Rowley Regis branch of the Independent Labour Party. Again speakers were organised, the chief being Wilfred Wellock, Labour candidate for Stourbridge, and Fred Longden, Labour candidate for Deritend, Birmingham.[56]

---

54 *Express and Star,* 1 and 2 May 1926.

55 *Express and Star,* 3 May 1926.

56 *Dudley Herald,* 8 May 1926.

The ad-hoc development of an organisation to implement the strike was evident in the provision of sports, entertainment and other activities to the strikers and others made idle. The T.U.C. Strike Committee considered this important for maintaining order, good humour and high morale.[57] When Bushbury Parish Church offered the full and free use of their Institute Association building to the workers, principally the local railwaymen, they created a committee to organise 'whist drives and other social activities'.[58]

---

57 Symons, pp.141-142.

58 *Express and Star,* 8 May 1926.

How Effective Were The Strikes?

Once the strike started, there was virtually no aspect of it which was not disputed by the two sides, in particular the effectiveness of the strikes in bringing men out, causing others to cease work and bringing business to a halt. Government and newspaper reports often emphasised the 'drift back to work' and the effectiveness of management and other workers in keeping firms operating during the strike. However, many commented on the lack of buses and trams on the streets and other, more local, signs, such as the lack of street lights in Tipton.[59] One objective measure that is available is the number of people who were registered unemployed. A set of figures on Unemployed for the Midlands was published by the Ministry of Labour and reported in the *Express and Star* on Wednesday, 12th May. For the week-ending 26th April, unemployed numbered 104,568 and short time working 30,524. Two weeks later these figures were 255,231 and 166,510 respectively, increases of 144% and 445%. The impact across the different areas of the Black Country appeared to be very consistent, with most areas reporting similar weekly increases of 50% to 75% in registered unemployed. These seem to suggest that the strikes were having a big effect, given that these numbers would not include men who were unemployed due to their being on strike.

Looking at specific unions and industries, at least after some days if not immediately, gives a similar picture of a highly effective strike. During Monday, 3rd May, the NUR sent a telegram to all

---

59 *Dudley Herald,* 8 May 1926.

its branches saying that the 'stoppage appears inevitable – unless we advise otherwise everyman must act on instructions already given. No trains of any kind are to be worked by our members'.[60] On Tuesday, 4th May, it was reported that there was practically a complete stoppage of all public transport services throughout England. Local management immediately made efforts to run trains and advised on 5th May that it was hoped that 'a skeleton service' would be run 'from the GWR station in Wolverhampton to Birmingham and Knowle' and that similar services would be run 'between Birmingham and Stourbridge'. In addition, arrangements had been made for 'charabancs and buses to be run in certain districts under police protection' to replace the trains.[61] On 6th May, it was reported that seven passenger trains 'will be run on the GWR line from Wolverhampton to Birmingham, and return, during the day' and two trains on the LMS line. Also, that 'trains will run between Birmingham and Stourbridge'. Finally, it was announced that 'some trains' would run between Shrewsbury and Wolverhampton.[62] Over the weekend, the numbers of trains that ran each day increased, but the numbers were always low, 'five in all …. from Walsall to Birmingham,[63] 'four additional trains from Stourbridge Junction' along with 'a Birmingham to London train' and 'a Chester to Wolverhampton train'.[64] Whilst some trains ran, and these were much applauded in the press, there were also hints that the services that did run were very slow and intermittent. It was commented that LMS ran a train from Birmingham to

---

60 *Express and Star*, 3 May 1926.

61 *Express and Star*, 5 May 1926.

62 *Express and Star*, 6 May 1926.

63 *Express and Star*, 7 May 1926.

64 *Express and Star*, 8 May 1926.

Wolverhampton on Thursday, 7th May, and that the assistant guard operated the gates at the crossings. As the train would have to stop at each crossing whilst the gates were operated, it definitely would have had many 'stops and starts' on its journey.[65]

The slow improvement in the service continued in the second week of the strike, but the numbers involved were still very small compared to the normal level of service. By Wednesday, 12th May, it was reported in the *Express and Star* that 50 different services were running. However, attempts were made to show a better service than actually existed by listing all the main line stations in operation, even if it was the same train that served them. So a service from London to Wolverhampton and then on to Crewe was reported as two trains, when in fact it was only one.[66]

A similar pattern is in evidence on the buses and trams. Across the Black Country, the strike by drivers and conductors was practically complete, with no buses or trams running. There were the same attempts to start a skeleton service as quickly as possible. On 4th May, the West Bromwich Government Emergency Committee decided to run a bus service with volunteers, primarily to provide transport to 'the many 100s of West Bromwich people who work in Birmingham'. A service to Colmore Row in Birmingham began on 5th May. Over the 6 days, 23,000 passengers were carried and 4,519 miles run. In addition, the council informed owners of charabancs that they could run their vehicles and ply for hire, and 'many did so'.[67] In Wolverhampton the strike was described as firm, so that nothing came from a meeting between the Wolverhampton Transport

---

65 *Dudley Herald,* 8 May 1926.

66 *Express and Star,* 10 May 1926.

67 *Minutes of West Bromwich Council meeting 7th July 1926,* Sandwell, Archive, CB-B/1/39.

Committee and representatives of the local transport workers with a view to running a skeleton service on 7th May.[68] However, preparations were being made in the first week to construct a 'volunteer motor bus service' and by 10th May, Owen Silvers, General Manager Of Wolverhampton Tramways Department and Road Transport Officer on the Government Emergency Committee, informed the *Express and Star* that a service was now 'well organised', but had 'yet to be sanctioned by Wolverhampton council. No tram service is contemplated until the buses are brought into operation'.[69] The following day, after the council sanction, which has been discussed earlier, ten buses were on the roads of Wolverhampton. The service started at 7:50am and each bus was manned by three men in plain clothes and a uniformed constable. Only seven routes were covered in all, three with two buses and four with one bus each.[70] The next day, Wednesday, 12th May, a '12 minute tram service between Dudley and Birmingham' was started at 5:00am, again with a police officer on each tram.[71] However, there were areas of the Black Country still without any buses and trams on 11th May, Brierley Hill being one of them.[72]

In other industries it was the large businesses that tended to attract the most attention in the newspapers, because of the high number of people involved. However, we can see from the reports a general pattern that must have applied to all businesses in the region. At the end of the first full day of the strike, Tuesday, 4th

---

68 *Express and Star*, 7 May 1926.

69 *Express and Star*, 10 May 1926.

70 *Express and Star*, 11 May 1926.

71 *Express and Star*, 12 May 1926.

72 Express and Star, 11 May 1926.

May, the iron and steel works of Stewarts and Lloyd at Coombe Wood in Halesowen closed down. 3,000 men signed on to the unemployment register at Cradley Heath on Wednesday. A week later the Cradley Heath Exchange reported an increase of almost 6,200 to a total of 10,000 claimants, mostly from Coombes Wood and Hingley's works and the mines in the area.[73]

One of the reasons for the difference of reported opinions for the effectiveness of the strike is obviously that of propaganda for each side. However, putting that aside, three factors were crucial in determining the effectiveness of the strikes on halting the operation of businesses. They were the proportion of workers in each business that went on strike, the supply of fuel, mainly coal, held on the premises, and, thirdly, access to transport for delivering supplies and shipping out finished goods. Each of these factors varied over the period of the General Strike, and by business, for a wide range of reasons.

The proportion of workers in a business on strike changed as different sets of workers were called out, volunteers and others replaced strikers and strikers 'drifted' back to work. Production of the *Express and Star* stopped completely at midnight on 3rd May, and only a short 'bulletin' was produced on the 4th. On following days, gestetner-copied editions were produced, becoming longer as the strike continued. This was because all the typographic workers went on strike and brought the printing presses to a complete halt. Whilst some journalists went on strike on the 6th, enough management and other staff were available to collate news items and use the hastily acquired gestetner machines. In contrast, at the Sunbeam Motor Company in Wolverhampton, when only 50 or 60 men from

---

73 *Dudley Herald,* 8 and 15 May 1926.

the A.E.U. were called out on strike, the works was reported as being 'well able to continue'. This changed when 2,500 went on strike shortly afterwards.[74]

The supply of fuel, which was mainly in the form of coal, was highly critical for some businesses in the Black Country. The *Dudley Herald* on Saturday, 8th May noted that the reports they were receiving from businesses at the end of the first week said that it was the supply of power which was 'the main determinant of whether they can work'. Messrs James Smellie Ltd, owned by the mayor of Dudley, reported that they were able to operate at capacity in the week just ending, but the following week 'depends on power'. Some businesses were almost immediately affected by the lack of fuel. The Earl of Dudley's Round Hill Works closed on Monday, 3rd May, with the exception of the 16 inch mill, whilst the Harts Hill ironworks, with the exception of the 'guide' mill, had closed on Saturday, 8th May. The Brettel Lane and Bradley Ironworks closed part way through the first week. At the same time, the iron and steel sections of the Patent Shaft and Axletree Company had 'run out of fuel and will remain closed until new supplies arrive'. Whilst work elsewhere in the company was found for some of the men, 'numbers of men' 'signed on' at the Employment Exchange.[75] The various glassworks in the Wordsley, Amblecote and Brierley Hill areas reported that they had 'sufficient fuel' in the first week. However, they also reported in the same edition of the *Express and Star* that they were 'very concerned because stocks of fuel are being rapidly used up and if the furnaces go out they have to be reconstructed'.[76]

---

74 *Express and Star*, 7 May 1926.

75 *Express and Star*, 3 May 1926.

76 *Express and Star*, 3 May 1926.

Electricity generation was highly dependent on coal, and some efforts were made to reduce the use of electricity in order to reduce pressure on the electricity generators. 'All the electric illuminated signs in the parish of Tipton have been put out.'.[77] However, there appeared to be confidence in being able to continue the supply. The Wolverhampton Borough Engineer, S. T. Allen, had 'no fear about being able to carry on despite a few men employed at the corporation electricity generating station having been called out'. A similar report was made about the West Bromwich Corporation Electric Works.[78] A lack of coal was never mentioned and indicates that, at least early in the strike, they were confident about continuing fuel supplies.

Some industries, mainly those less dependent upon fuel, found that transport to be the major cause for concern. The Willenhall lock makers were reported to be in full operation during the first week of the strike, their only difficulty being transporting finished articles to customers. By the middle of the following week many of them had ceased working due to this difficulty and having nowhere in their premises to store the articles, an early example of how a 'just in time' methodology is vulnerable to disruption at any point in the process.[79] On Monday, 3rd May, the Wolverhampton postmaster general made a public announcement asking the 'public to refrain from using the services. No parcels or letters greater than 8oz in weight or batches of advertising material will be accepted for delivery, due to restrictions on the use of railways for the transport of mail'. Later in the week, it was announced that 'postal services are

---

77 *Dudley Herald,* 8 May 1926.

78 *Express and Star,* 11 May 1926. *Dudley Herald,* 15 May 1926.

79 *Dudley Herald,* 8 and 15 May 1926.

down to two per day' and 'mail boxes will be cleared by 4:00pm rather than 6:00pm'.[80] Transport problems could have a wide ranging effect. Retail businesses in Dudley reported lower sales on Saturday, which they attributed to a lack of public transport.[81] Beattie's in Wolverhampton wanted to dispel rumours of low stocks by placing an advert in the *Express and Star* saying that this was 'absurdly untrue; on the contrary, the fact is that the Beattie Store is heavily stocked in every department with all the Best. The Strike has threatened for months and we have secured ample stocks to meet all demands for three months.'[82] The company presenting *'Jazz Marriage'* at the Wolverhampton Grand Theatre was unable to fulfil its engagement 'owing to transport difficulties', 'for the first time ever for this cause in the history of the theatre'.[83]

However, it also appears that some businesses benefited from the disruption. With demand exceeding supply, the costs of renting motor vehicles increased. Cycle shops and dealers reported a 'sustained demand for clothes', speculating that it was 'probably as people move from rail, tram and bus transport to petrol driven transport'. Wireless retailers also reported 'good business'.[84]

---

80 *Express and Star,* 3, 7 and 8 May 1926.

81 *Dudley Herald,* 15 May 1926.

82 *Express and Star,* 8 May 1926.

83 *Express and Star,* 8 May 1926.

84 *Dudley Herald,* 8 and 15 May 1926.

How Loyal Were The Men To The Unions?

The question of how loyal the men were to their unions was continually raised on both sides. It appears that, at least initially, the men were very loyal. When the Vehicle Builders' Union and the A.E.U. called men out at the Sunbeam Motor Company, 2,500 left work and operations came to a standstill. Similarly, at the Star Engineering Company, the works was closed despite 50% of the men not being trade unionists. It was reported that about 140 union men remained at work. However, these may have been charge hands and foundry men who were in different unions and not called out at that time.[85] Owen Silvers, the Wolverhampton Government Emergency Committee Road Officer, commented that [the tramways men's] attitude 'so far seemed fairly united' and three days later that 'at the present there are only two who have returned' and 'they are not drivers'.[86] A notice at the G.W.R. works in Stafford Street, Wolverhampton, announced that 'wages cannot be paid this week because 80% of the railway clerks are on strike'.[87]

After the weekend of 8th and 9th May and their visits to Wolverhampton and district, William Whiteley and Robert Wilson, Labour MPs for Blaydon, County Durham and Jarrow respectively, reported that they had seen no troops, that not a bus or tram was running, and that spirits were high. They

---

85 *Express and Star,* 6 and 7 May 1926.

86 *Express and Star,* 7 and 10 May 1926.

87 *Express and Star,* 7 May 1926.

reported that the workers declared that 'they are out to win'.[88] The Wolverhampton Trades and Labour Council Emergency Committee noted that on Monday 10th, the manager of the local Labour Exchange said that 35,000 workers had ceased work in Wolverhampton. It thought there was a 'general sense that the trade union movement stood solid and were prepared to fight to the bitter end in support of the miners'. They found that the non-union men, as well as union men, 'answered the call' to strike in support of the miners.[89] Even as the General Strike was ending, solidarity appeared to remain high. At a meeting of railwaymen at the Crown Hotel, Dudley, Oliver Baldwin, son of the prime minister Stanley Baldwin and Labour candidate for Dudley, said that 'he was amazed at the solidarity of the Dudley workmen in the dispute. Dudley had always been a Tory Trade Union area and it was refreshing for a reformer to see the transformation the strike had brought about'.[90] As measured by the numbers of men who assembled at meetings, works gates and town centres, support for the strike was large and widespread. Reports in the local newspapers often referred to 'huge crowds in Princes Square' in Wolverhampton at different times, and 'masses of workers demonstrated' in Bilston. Even when men decided not to go on strike, they could support it in different ways. The Old Hill and district branch of the Union of House Painters and Decorators decided to open a distress fund for strikers and their families.[91]

In evaluating the strike, Postgate, Wilkinson and Horrabin allocated areas to four classes. Class I was towns where response

---

88 Symons, p.196.

89 *Wolverhampton Trades and Labour Council Report*, Warwick, Modern Records Centre, MSS.292/252.62/5/52.

90 *Express and Star*, 13 May 1926.

91 *Dudley Herald*, 15 May 1926.

was near to 100 per cent. Class II was where the strike was wholly effective but with weaknesses in some sections. Class Ill was towns with serious weaknesses. Class IV was towns where the strike broke down. Wolverhampton was class I; Smethwick, Stourbridge, Walsall and Wednesbury were class II.[92] However, support was not always unequivocal. Early in the strike, the Cradley Heath chainmakers met to discuss the strike and decided they would continue to work, the reason being that they had a three month's agreement with the employers, and if they went on a 'lightening strike' the employers might propose a 'reduction in wages' afterwards. It should be noted that the ever active Charles Sitch met with the Chainmakers Union at the Cradley Heath Workers' Institute. This time his influence failed to persuade the men to support the strike.[93]

Conversely, the newspapers often mentioned that there were men who 'drifted back to work'. The government encouraged the men to return to work by guaranteeing that the 'financial interests of trade unionists who remain at or return to work shall be protected when conflict ends'. This was seen by the employers to be an important tool to use against the strike. The Birmingham, Wolverhampton and Stafford District of the Engineering and Allied Employers Association asked for the government to clarify their position. A telegram from Patrick Hannon, Conservative MP for Birmingham Moseley, replied, stating explicitly that trade unionists would be protected, if they went back to work of their own volition.[94]

Even so, for this tactic to be successful in undermining the

---

92 : http://wolvestuc.org.uk/index.php/wbdtuc/our-history?showall=&start=5 [accessed 9 February 2017].

93 *Dudley Herald,* 8 and 15 May 1926.

94 *Express and Star,* 10 May 1926.

impact of the strike, the management had to be very active with the men at a business level. A meeting of about 250 employees of Guy Motors, with two trade union representatives, was addressed by Sidney Guy, the managing director, where he assured them that 'there would be no reduction in wages, no matter what happened to the mining industry'. A secret ballot was held and a majority of 75% was in favour of resuming duty at the start of the next day's shift. This figure is disputed by the trade union representatives, who said that only a minority of workers attended the meeting. Certainly this seems to be a small proportion of the total number employed. However, Sidney Guy said that this was because union pickets prevented more entering the building. Whatever the truth, it was reported that 87 re-started that day, out of a total workforce of about 1,000. By the next day it was reported that '447 men out of 800' were back at work, suggesting that a substantial 'drift back to work' did take place.[95]

Clarity on the scale of the drift back to work is difficult to gather, mainly because both sides had an interest in either presenting a bigger or smaller movement than actually took place. For example, on 10th May, it was reported that '78% of the moulders at the Sunbeam Motor Company returned to work this morning'. 'There are a few men at work in every department' and 'more men would have returned, but they lived at a distance and could not get to work'. However, moulders were only a small number of the total on strike, approximately 115 in all, and no indication is given of the level or craft of the men at work.[96] Further, these may have been relatively isolated events given prominence by the newspapers, because it was noted that,

---

95 *Express and Star,* 10 and 12 May 1926.

96 *Express and Star,* 12 May 1926, reworked figures.

other than the Guy Motors and Sunbeam Motor Company works, there was 'no change for the motor industry in Wolverhampton'.[97] However, other industries were also reportedly affected by a 'drift back to work'. It was reported that the 250 men of the Iron and Steel Workers' Confederation, who went on strike on 4th May at the Wolverhampton Works of Bayliss, Jones and Bayliss, had a meeting and ballot and decided by a large majority to return to work the next day. Forty men on the manufacturing side had already returned to work. Similarly 200 builders employed on the construction of the Courtaulds' factory in Wolverhampton, who had been on strike, returned to work on 10th May.[98] Whatever the scale, it is clear that there was a drift amongst both union and non-union men.

The effectiveness and role of those who assisted in the government's arrangements was another disputed subject. According to the government they were 'volunteers', but the strikers saw them as 'strike breakers'. Also, the exact nature of the volunteering was open to debate. A notice calling for volunteers from the Wolverhampton Volunteer Service Committee stated that 'arrangements for pay will be made according to the duties performed'.[99] In West Bromwich, when the Corporation Electricity drivers, stokers and labourers stopped work at 7:00am on Tuesday, 11th May, volunteers were quickly found and started work immediately so that there was 'no effect on operations'. However, it appears that the volunteers were paid the ordinary rate of wages for the work, plus 10 shillings a day, a sizeable increase in pay

---

97 *Express and Star*, 12 May 1926.

98 *Express and Star*, 10 May 1926.

99 *Express and Star*, 3 May 1926.

for labouring men.[100] The payment of the special and temporary constables was viewed as a political opportunity by those supporting the strike. It was raised in a meeting of the Wolverhampton Town Council by a Labour member, who asked 'whether it was true that a special constable received as much in wages in two days as a miner in a week?'.[101] On 12th May, Wolverhampton's chief constable confirmed that 'over 600 special constables in Wolverhampton' were not paid, but temporary constables were paid.

How effective the calls for volunteers were appears unclear. According to the *Express and Star,* 'hundreds are enlisting at Wolverhampton'.[102] By 7th May, there had been 'about 1,000 volunteers' but 'only a small number have been called to assist'. In Walsall, it was reported that 'another 1,000 hands have signed on making 2,000 new signatures in the past few days, with recruits mainly from the fancy leather trade'.[103] There may have been an element of propaganda in these reports because the Walsall mayor, David Parry, at the council meeting on 10th May, reported that 'up to the end of Saturday there had been 884 volunteers, plus special constables'.[104] Whilst on 7th May in the *Express and Star,* a spokesman for the Wolverhampton Corporation Tramways Department is reported as saying that 'no volunteers had offered their services' and a Wolverhampton 'transport authority' is quoted as saying that the 'list of volunteer motor drivers is …. disappointing. None have been called upon, but if they were

---

100 *Minutes of West Bromwich Council meetings 7th July 1926,* Sandwell, Archive, CB-B/1/39.

101 *Minutes Of Meeting Of Wolverhampton Council,* Wolverhampton, Archive, LS/L352.

102 *Express and Star,* 4 May 1926.

103 *Express and Star,* 8 May 1926.

104 *Express and Star,* 11 May 1926.

needed there were not enough'. Perhaps an element of reality was being reported by the *Dudley Herald* on 8th May, when Bilston district reported that the response to an appeal for volunteers was 'fair'. It may be that workers who were laid off by businesses affected by the strike saw the calls for volunteers as a way of supplementing or replacing the small benefits offered by the state and the Poor Law Unions. Walsall's reported volunteering rate matches the reported impact of the strike on the town's main industry, with the numbers in the second week of the strike showing substantial increases compared to the first week.

Strike breaking came in many different guises, again depending upon the observers' position on the General Strike. Miners tried to prevent 'coal picking', whereby individuals searched for coal from easily accessible seams, or in the many slag heaps dotted around the region. It was thought that this practice extended the 1921 strike and made it harder for the miners to place pressure on the mine owners. However, it was reported that 'coal picking is taking place across Dudley by men, women and children' and that the coal was being 'hawked from door to door'.[105] The *Express and Star* noted that this was being done 'mainly by miners on strike', and that they were charging a shilling per hundredweight, a substantial discount to the price on the rationed market.[106] Others took advantage of the situation in more informal ways. It would appear that lorry drivers were charging for giving people lifts to work. Consequently, 'Many women who live in Rowley Regis and work in Birmingham and who cannot afford the cost charged by lorry drivers for a lift are walking to and from work.'[107]

---

105 *Dudley Herald*, 8 and 15 May 1926.

106 *Express and Star*, 8 May 1926.

107 *Dudley Herald*, 8 May 1926.

That is not to say that there were no altruistic actions recorded during the General Strike, but even they appear to have been controversial. The Wolverhampton branch of the National Council of Women posted an advertisement in the *Express and Star* 'asking owners of cars willing to give lifts between 7:30am and 9:30am and 5:30pm to 7:30pm to communicate with Mrs A. N. Tomlins, Astolat, Tettenhall. Employers can assist by sending names and addresses of employees needing assistance.'[108] This appears to have been a spontaneous offer without remuneration as far as the National Council of Women is concerned. At their May meeting on the 28th, the chairman (sic) asked for retrospective approval 'of the action of several members of the Executive Committee during the General Strike'. It was explained that several members of the Executive Committee had held a meeting by telephone 'to organise means whereby business women and girls might be conveyed to and from work during the strike'. However, a Mrs Dale 'moved that the proceedings were unconstitutional and should not have been taken except with the consent of the Executive Committee'. A vote was held and three voted against the retrospective approval. Numbers voting in favour were not given, but other meetings that year had 60 to 80 members attending, so it is likely to have been substantial. Mrs Dale was on the Executive Committee, so it may be that she objected to the procedure adopted rather than the action itself.[109]

However, not everything was controversial. There were reports of 'friendly lifts in private cars' having been 'offered to those having to walk to work in Bilston.'[110] Other drivers were

---

108 *Express and Star*, 10 May 1926.

109 *Minute Book of the National Council Of Women April 1924 to December 1931*, Wolverhampton, Archive D-SO-8/3/2.

110 *Dudley Herald*, 8 May 1926.

reported to have placed 'a collection box in their cars' for donations to 'local hospitals'.[111] Businesses also made arrangements for their employees to travel to work, especially where they had more than one site within the area. It was reported that Cable Accessories Ltd and other businesses were using their company vans to move their employees to work between Wolverhampton and Birmingham.[112] The summary of the General Strike actions at the West Bromwich Council meeting noted that 'private car owners gave lifts when they were travelling and made special trips to give people lifts between West Bromwich and Birmingham, of course, free of charge'.[113]

---

111 *The Birmingham Post Saturday* 8 May 1926, Sandwell, Archive, EPH/A/561.

112 *Dudley Herald*, 15 May 1926.

113 *Minutes of West Bromwich Council meeting 7th July 1926*, Sandwell, Archive, CB-B/1/39.

The Role Of Public Meetings

As the strike progressed, public meetings and processions became even more of a feature. The Wolverhampton Trades Council organised 'open air meetings' every day at the Market Place, arranging for locals and miners' representatives from Cannock to be regular speakers.[114] Distance appeared to be no difficulty for the strikers. On Friday, 7th May, processions were arranged from what was described as the 'central headquarters of the strikers, the Labour Club' in Wolverhampton to Bloxwich and Wednesbury.[115] At a West Bromwich open air meeting, it was noted that one of the banners on display was from the Wolverhampton branch of the National Union of Railwaymen.[116] For those travelling from some distance the occasion was often very well organised. A 'large contingent marched in order from Tipton' to a meeting at the Fair Ground in Trindle Road Dudley on Sunday, 9th May.[117] However, some of the public meetings were probably meant to be more local in their scope. Strikers in Tipton gathered at the Wellington Inn, their headquarters, on the night of Friday, 14th May and marched around the parish. Singing and music were often a major component of the meeting or procession. The Tipton procession included the singing of 'hymns and songs to a piano accompaniment'. Unfortunately, it

---

114 *Wolverhampton Trades and Labour Council Report*, Warwick, Modern Records Centre, MSS.292/252.62/5/52.

115 *Express and Star*, 7 May 1926.

116 *West Bromwich Free Press: 'Strike Bulletin', No. 1 and 2,* Sandwell, Archive, BS-KJ/8/3/5.

117 *Dudley Herald*, 15 May 1926.

was not described how they arranged for the piano to travel in the procession.[118]

Speakers were the central feature of all public meetings, and at many of the large ones, some of them came from outside the region. Ellen Wilkinson, MP for Middlesbrough East, addressed a 'large crowd of strikers in the Wolverhampton Market Square' on Friday, 7th May, where she 'spoke in optimistic vein of the strike', after Robert Wilson, MP for Jarrow, opened the proceedings.[119] Included on the platform were William Whiteley MP, Oswald Mosley, William Brown, Labour candidate for Wolverhampton West, and Robert Williams, Labour candidate for Wolverhampton East.[120]

Large numbers were important in enforcing the strike, showing disapproval at certain decisions and countering the actions of the Government Emergency Committees in maintaining public services. A meeting in Brierley Hill attracted 'between 5,000 and 6,000 men'. It was called in protest over 'the Minister of Labour disallowing the claims of 1,500 iron and steel workers for unemployment pay on the grounds that they were not totally unemployed on 3rd May.'[121] It appears that the union leaders hoped that the mere presence of large numbers of pickets, or a large public meeting, would be sufficient to press their case. However, it is clear that their effect was limited, mainly due to the trade union leaders' desire not to cause trouble with the police and authorities. On 5th May, C. J. James attempted to run a charabanc from his garage in Sweetman Street, Wolverhampton, and 'a number of men picketed' his

---

118 *Dudley Herald*, 15 May 1926.

119 *Express and Star,* 7 and 8 May 1926.

120 Lansbury Weekly.

121 *Express and Star*, 8 May 1926.

garage, whilst a charabanc was stopped in Stafford Street in Wolverhampton on the same afternoon. In both instances the 'police arrived in time to prevent any disturbance'.[122] A crowd of 'nearly 1,000 assembled in Cleveland Street, Wolverhampton, in the evening' where they 'thronged the road and held up traffic'. Foot police, with three mounted specials, under the direction of the chief constable, David Webster, 'contained the crowd to the pavement', from where they 'cheered' a bus which 'left the depot at about 7:30pm'. People began to disperse, but at 9:00pm, groups numbering several hundred in total still remained.[123] Again, the following morning, 'dense crowds of strikers assembled in Queen Square, Wolverhampton'. Police were able to keep them to the pavements, from where they gave 'ironical cheers to passing buses'. Without clear objectives and instructions for action, the crowds appeared 'listless' and tended to drift away as the day progressed.[124] Similarly, when it became known that goods were being moved from the railway station in Wolverhampton on 7th May, pickets arrived, but did not intervene. There was 'no disorder' and the goods were removed. Perhaps the fact that the goods were 'perishable' affected the pickets' actions. However, similar incidents were reported at Old Hill and Cradley stations, where 'large crowds gathered but did not interfere' and it appears the goods were not perishable.[125] Tramway and train strikers gathered at the railway depot in Bilston in 'fairly large numbers' when word went around that goods were to be moved by volunteer drivers,

---

122 *Express and Star*, 5 May 1926.

123 *Express and Star*, 10 May 1926.

124 *Express and Star*, 11 May 1926.

125 *Express and Star*, 7 May 1926.

with a police escort. Despite a number of journeys being made, 'there was no attempt to molest them'.[126] When there was enough disorder to warrant an arrest, it was very low key, considering the numbers involved. In Dudley, a 'considerable crowd attempted to interrupt the passage of a char-a-banc containing workers returning home'. The vehicle eventually proceeded on its way and, later, 'police had trouble with one young man in the crowd who was arrested on a charge of assaulting a police officer'.[127] This series of actions and responses continued until the end of the strike. On the afternoon of 12th May, 'large crowds' gathered in Queen Square, Wolverhampton, due to buses operated by volunteers. There was only one small incident reported, which had no effect on the buses. Later, when the 'crowd interfered with traffic', police 'attended to clear the road way'.[128]

Attempts to enforce the strike could also be on a small scale, and involve women as well. In Rowley Regis, according to the *Express and Star*, a canal boat was delivering bricks to Doulton's Pottery Works when it was 'held up by a small body of men assisted by women'. The boat 'was let through but warned they would not be allowed through again'. Again, the same pattern of not wanting to confront the authorities directly was apparent, so when police 'attended the scene', the 'group moved off'.

Strikers did develop a number of different tactics other than large scale picketing to attempt to enforce the stoppage. In Dudley, Midland Red busmen from the Harts Hill depot rode a motor cycle in front of a bus to slow it down, then pickets would climb onto

---

126 *Express and Star*, 11 May 1926.

127 *Express and Star*, 7 May 1926.

128 *Express and Star*, 12 May 1926.

the bus and 'persuade the passengers to disembark'.[129] A variation of this tactic was reported to be in use in West Bromwich and Stourbridge. A group of men would board a bus and fill it, and then to refuse to pay their fares. Drivers would continue along the route until they saw a policeman, where they stopped the bus. The policeman would advise the men to pay their fares. If they still refused, the driver would announce that he was going to the nearest police station, at which point the men 'scampered off'. At the very least, this would have delayed the service, and prevented others from using the bus.[130] Damaging buses was widely reported elsewhere in the country, but not in the Black Country. Barriers were placed on railway lines and road. A goods train driver who, 'passing through Portobello found that the gates were fastened against him, continued his journey by crashing through them'.[131] On Saturday, 8th May, a charabanc carrying workers from Birmingham to Blackheath 'crashed through a plank placed in the road at Quinton by strikers and continued on its way'.[132] There may very well have been other examples of this type of action which were not reported in the newspapers, because both of these incidents record a very un-orthodox response by the driver.

There are also examples of the use of the 'presence' of a public meeting to persuade workers to go on strike being unsuccessful. Strikers assembled near the Salter Works in West Bromwich where approximately 2,000 men worked. No speeches were made and there was no interference with the workers as they came and went over the lunch time period. There is no report of the

---

129 *Dudley Herald*, 8 May 1926.

130 *Dudley Herald*, 15 May 1926.

131 *Express and Star*, 10 May 1926.

132 *Express and Star*, 8 May 1926.

workers going on strike. Given that the Mayor, Thomas Cottrell, and Alderman Bache, both very much against the General Strike, were present with a body of policemen, and they spoke to the organisers, but made no attempt to disperse the men, it can be assumed that their 'presence' had little effect on the workers.[133] A similar action took place at the Globe Tube Works in Wednesbury. A group of men attempted to 'induce the workers to strike'. However, 'police attended and the group were prevailed upon to disperse'.[134] The same incident was reported in the *Dudley Herald*: an un-named 'local trade union leader' attempted to 'close the Globe Tube Works, by marching in procession a band of strikers to the works gate as the shift was ending'. However, it was unsuccessful because 'the eloquence of the speakers failed to impress the men who remained loyal to the works'. There is no mention in the *Dudley Herald* about how the event concluded, but there is agreement in the reports that 'a large body of police who were on hand were not used'.[135]

Another objective for large public meetings was to communicate various messages. How effective these meetings were for communication purposes must be open to some doubt. It was noted that Robert Wilson, when he spoke in the Wolverhampton Market Place on 7th May, was 'almost inaudible because of the noise from the market'.[136] Space limited how many people could hear the speakers at the bigger events. When Ellen Wilkinson and others visited Wolverhampton over the weekend of 8th and 9th May, so many people wanted to hear them speak

---

133 'Strike Bulletin', No. 1 and 2, Sandwell, Archive, BS-KJ/8/3/5.
134 *Express and Star*, 11 May 1926.
135 *Dudley Herald*, 15 May 1926.
136 *Express and Star*, 8 May 1926.

at the Theatre Royal that an overflow meeting was held at the Cooperative Hall. 1,100 heard Mosley, Robert Wilson and Robert Williams speak there, but 'many thousands' were not able to gain entrance to the venues, and so 'stood outside in the rain'.[137] However, the large number of meetings across the Black Country meant that messages could be repeated, both to the attendees and to the leaders of the General Strike. In all the meetings the men were asked to 'keep calm'. Communication could also be from the men to the leaders. At the West Bromwich Labour Party May Day meeting and a meeting in West Bromwich on the following Tuesday, a resolution was passed 'appreciating the magnificent lead given by the General Council' of the T.U.C..[138]

It is clear that some of the authorities were worried about public meetings and attempted to restrict them. West Bromwich Borough Council Mayor, Thomas Cottrell, prohibited all processions, under the emergency powers legislation.[139] A procession organised by Walter Maybury and others through the town on Saturday, 8th May, intended to end with speeches at a piece of waste ground on the edge of the town centre, was 'forming and on the point of starting'. Chief Superintendent Tucker told Walter Maybury that the Mayor and the Chief of Police had decided under the Emergency Powers Act that the procession 'should not proceed'. Despite some of the crowd wanting the procession to go ahead, Maybury cancelled it and immediately started the following meeting.[140] Other local authorities were less openly hostile to these meetings, or used

---

137 Lansbury Weekly.

138 'Strike Bulletin', No. 1 and 2. Sandwell, Archive, BS-KJ/8/3/5. *Dudley Herald* 15 May 1926.

139 *Minutes of West Bromwich Council meeting 7th July 1926*, Sandwell, Archive, CB-B/1/39.

140 'Strike Bulletin', No. 1 and 2. Sandwell, Archive, BS-KJ/8/3/5.

more subtle excuses for moving them away from the centre of towns. A mass meeting was called for Halesowen on Tuesday, 11th May and men 'poured' into the main thoroughfare of the town. The police, to relieve traffic congestion, advised that the meeting be held at Cornbow, a little way from the centre, where the meeting would not be interrupted.[141] Communist meetings attracted special attention from the authorities, based on their concerns about the influence on trade unions of the Soviet Union, through the Communist Party of Great Britain. A meeting on 4th May of about 800 people at the Wolverhampton Market Place, with McManus, chairman of the Communist Party of Great Britain, as a key speaker, was immediately dispersed by the police, which implies a measure of violence in the process.[142]

How mass public meetings were called in an environment where the strikers did not have easy access to mass communication is hinted at in the report of a meeting in Halesowen on 11th May. During the day, messages were 'circulated' in Cradley Heath, Old Hill, Cradley and Netherton, an area about 1.5 miles across, that a mass meeting of strikers was to be held in Halesowen that evening. Presumably this means that it was mainly done by word of mouth, possibly assisted by motor cycle messengers for the outlying areas.[143]

Public meetings were perceived to be important to both sides in the dispute for a variety of reasons. Another important consideration for both the government and the trade unions was the supply of essentials, mainly coal and food, to the population in general. Both sides wanted to show that they were in control

---

141 *Dudley Herald*, 15 May 1926.

142 http://wolvestuc.org.uk/index.php/wbdtuc/our-history?showall=&start=5 [accessed 9 February 2017].

143 *Dudley Herald*, 15 May 1926.

of the situation, and therefore issued separate permits to allow the movement of these goods about the region. At the same time, for obvious reasons, the striking miners did not want coal to be too easily available to the employers and other industrial users of coal.

The Supply Of Fuel And Food

At a national level, at the start of the strike, industry had coal supplies for only a week. However, what turned out to be an optimistic report from the Dudley area stated that 'most local firms have laid on heavy stocks in case of a general coal strike'. The Round Oak steel works was specifically reported to have 'six weeks' stock of coal'[144], although, it was thought, some of it would have to be kept for starting up as soon as the strike was ended. This situation was reflected elsewhere in the Black Country by the speed with which works consuming large quantities of coal shut down at least part of their operations within the first week.[145] In the Wolverhampton area, it was reported that there were only 1,250 tons of coal and 500 tons of slack. Some firms reported very low levels of coal, because supplies from the collieries had ceased on Friday, 30th April. It appears that businesses had made few preparations for a miners' strike until the last week of April. Mines in Cannock and Hednesfield reported heavy demands just before the strike began. At the same time, mine owners began to make preparations for the strike by restricting sales, so as to keep a supply of coal to operate their water pumps. The Earl of Dudley's Baggeridge Collieries reported that 'fuel stocks of 4,707 tons at 31st December 1925 were practically cleared before the strike'.[146]

Across the region reports soon arrived that there were shortages of coal. Brierley Hill was typical in reporting that, on 1st May,

---

144 *Express and Star,* 1 May 1926.

145 *Express and Star,* 1 May 1926.

146 *Earl Of Dudley's Baggeridge Colliery Ltd Half Year Report 1926,* Dudley, Archive, DE/7/2/2/3.

'local dealers' held only 'small stocks'.[147] Therefore, rationing was quickly introduced. As usual, the government was much more fully prepared than the unions for this situation. For industrial users, the ration was based on the quantity of coal used in the four weeks prior to 1st May and the quantity of coal they had on their premises. They were limited to 50% of the previous four weeks' average weekly usage. They were allowed to consume more than this for either two weeks or until they had used 50% of the stock of coal on their premises, whichever came sooner. Factories that wanted to continue using more than their permitted level of coal had to apply for a special permit from the local Coal Officer.[148] Householders with more than 5cwt of coal were not allowed further deliveries until their stocks were exhausted. The ration was then 1cwt per household per week. Exceptions were allowed for illness or if the household was unusually large. It was an offence for a coal dealer to deliver more than 1cwt of coal to a household, with both the dealer and the householder being liable to prosecution. It was also an offence for a householder to register with more than one dealer. The seriousness of the shortage of coal was reflected in the decision later in the first week, Thursday, 6th May, to reduce the household ration by half for all grades of fuel, coal, slack and coke.[149] Inevitably this placed a lot of pressure on the system of permits. The Dudley Coal Officer's premises at the public library had 'many women with babes in arms' queuing for permits.[150]

The situation was either changing very quickly or the early reports about the position of coal supplies in the region were

---

147 *Express and Star,* 1 May 1926.

148 *Dudley Herald,* 8 May 1926.

149 *Express and Star,* 6 May 1926.

150 *Dudley Herald,* 8 May 1926.

inaccurate. Early reports were that certain 'institutions', amongst them the Wolverhampton General Hospital, the Commercial Road electricity power station and the Bilston gas works, had made special provisions for fuel and had 'adequate supplies', but 'strict economy will be practised'. For the hospital, that meant only accident and emergency cases would be dealt with.[151] Adequate supplies appear to have been reckoned at 'three or four weeks' worth'.[152] However, in the newspapers, quantities varied widely. The *Express and Star* reported on 1st May that the Mond Gas Works in Dudley had coal for 'at least three months', whilst the *Dudley Herald* reported on 8th May that it had 'enough fuel for 12 months'. Similarly, the first reported announcement by the Brierley Hill Coal Officer, Councillor T. Williams, was that stocks of coal were 'very satisfactory'.[153] However, the *Express and Star* reported on the same day that 'stocks are running low and care needs to be taken in all areas'.[154]

By the middle of the second week of the strike the situation was quickly deteriorating. Wolverhampton coal merchants and dealers were 'rapidly becoming exhausted and many will be closed down this week if no supplies from outside the district are forthcoming'. The Fuel Officer was expecting supplies to arrive 'this week', and merchants and dealers had been asked at the end of Tuesday, 11th May to submit a 'return on stock levels by first post Wednesday'. He also announced that those who did not supply the return would receive 'no further supplies'.[155]

---

151 *Express and Star*, 6 May 1926.

152 *Express and Star*, 1 May 1926.

153 *Dudley Herald*, 8 May 1926.

154 *Express and Star*, 8 May 1926.

155 *Express and Star*, 11 May 1926.

It appears that supplies did arrive from outside the district by the end of the week, but these were 'the last allocation of fuel to Wolverhampton and District... after that there is no more except from local sources.'[156] It does appear that some areas were better supplied than others. Kingswinford Rural Council Coal Committee reported that stocks of coal were 'sufficient for several weeks.'.[157] It may be that, being a more rural area, other sources of fuel were more easily available than in industrial and urban areas. Or it might be that larger supplies of coal had been built up before the strike.

It appears that some businesses were in a better situation than others and businesses were better placed than householders. Various firms in the Dudley area, including T. E. Slater Ltd, Charles Lathe Ltd and Messrs Allen, reported that they had sufficient fuel for three months, which allowed arrangements to be made for coal to be distributed to Quarry Bank households from nearby works, 'not of the usual quality, but at a lower price'. By 13th May, most Wolverhampton merchants had 'no stocks of coal, but they have coke and slack'. Therefore, the scheme to supply households with coal from local businesses was extended to Wolverhampton.[158] The local Government Emergency Committee in Wednesbury found that there were little stocks in their area, and they also were 'asking those with coal stocks to release them for use'. By these means, the Mayor was 'sure that the problem can be surmounted.'.[159] In Bilston, the management of Hinkman's Springvale works decided that it

---

156 *Express and Star*, 14 May 1926.

157 *Dudley Herald*, 15 May 1926.

158 *Express and Star*, 11 to 13 May 1926.

159 *Express and Star*, 14 May 1926.

would not be possible for them to re-start until the miners were back at work and coal stocks replaced. Therefore, they agreed a 'reasonable price' with the Bilston Emergency Coal Committee for their remaining coal stocks. 'Carts and barrows were available to take the coal'.[160] This deterioration in supply also seemed to apply to electricity and gas supplies. It was reported by the fuel office at Union Street in Willenhall that 'all the requests for power had been coped with' in the first week. However, 'rationing will take place with some firms working the first three days of next week and others the last three days', but this 'all depended upon the amount of fuel available'.[161]

Although not mentioned in the press specifically, there does appear to have been an increase in retail prices of coal at the start of the strike. The Earl of Dudley's Baggeridge collieries increased the price of their coal by 20%, from 30 to 36 shillings per ton at wharves. There was some criticism regarding the increase, but Vincent Wickes, the colliery general manager, was 'quite able to justify it'.[162] Price increases must have been widespread and some, if not all, passed on to consumers, because, on Thursday, 13th May, Wolverhampton's Coal Government Emergency Committee stated that they had fixed prices at those charged by the Cooperative Society in Wolverhampton, 'as this was a fair average', and, especially, it limited the scope for profiteering.[163] Some councils appeared to have considered this issue at the beginning of the General Strike. Bilston Borough Council passed a resolution that, along with the circulation of the coal regulations to dealers, there

---

160 *Express and Star*, 14 May 1926.

161 *Express and Star*, 8 May 1926.

162 Dudley, Archive, DE/7/2/2/3.

163 *Express and Star*, 13 May 1926.

should be a recommendation that they 'make no increase in the price of present stocks of coal'.[164] In some areas, prices began to be reviewed after each major delivery to the area.[165]

Inevitably, with shortages and price rises, tempers flared on occasions, and antagonism was expressed by the public to coal merchants and dealers. 'A Dudley coal dealer has been very audibly saying he will suspend his business until conditions improve because he has been anathematised by people' he had sold coal to.[166] In addition, some people used illegal methods to acquire coal. Reports of coal being stolen increased, despite the difficulty in carrying it away.[167]

The experience of food supplies was almost the complete opposite from that of coal and fuel. Neither unions nor the government wanted to compromise the provision of food supplies to the public. Mr Jenkin, from the Dockers' Union, stated at a meeting of the T.U.C. that they would 'maintain by voluntary arrangement the distribution of essential foodstuffs'.[168] The experience was that food stuffs were rarely held up by the strike in the Black Country. William Kidson, of G. H. Kidson Ltd, a wholesale provision merchant and member of the Food Government Emergency Committee for Wolverhampton and District, reported that there were sufficient stocks to last several weeks. In Walsall, it was reported that local tradesmen 'have, of their own volition, ensured they have good stocks of supplies'.[169]

---

164 *Bilston Council minutes 3rd May 1926 Special Council Meeting,* Wolverhampton, Archive, LS/LB352/3.

165 *Express and Star,* 15 to 19 May 1926.

166 *Dudley Herald,* 22 May 1926.

167 *Dudley Herald,* 8 May 1926.

168 *Express and Star,* 1 May 1926.

169 *Express and Star,* 1 May 1926.

Local food businesses operated as normal. Willenhall bakers published notices of when people could send their meat and other items to the bake-houses to be cooked.[170] By the end of the first week, reports coming from 'all parts [of the] Midlands' indicated that there were 'ample food supplies' which 'precludes the necessity for rationing'.[171] This remained unchanged over the duration of the strike. On 12th May, Walsall's local Food Officer, Victor Crooke, reported that 'food supplies were normal', food lorries were not being interfered with, prices were being monitored, with price increases small and in line with the extra cost of transport, and 'merchants are selling only normal quantities to people to prevent hoarding'. The food committees were quickly wound down after the General Strike ended. Walsall's Area Food Government Emergency Committee last met on Thursday, 20th May.[172]

---

170 *Express and Star*, 12 May 1926.

171 *Express and Star*, 6 May 1926.

172 *Express and Star*, 8 to 18 May 1926.

Reporting The General Strike

At the beginning of the General Strike, many trade unionists thought they had scored a major victory by closing down the newspaper industry. West Bromwich Councillor, Joe Bailey, was reflecting a typical thought when he said they had removed from the government one of its most powerful weapons, 'The lying capitalist press'.[173] It was recognised by both sides that communication to the general public was going to be crucial in the strike, and that a lack of information was likely to encourage the spreading of rumours. The government responded with the *British Gazette,* and enforced a law against the spreading of 'false news'. The trade unions through the T.U.C. issued the *British Worker*. Local Trades Councils or Emergency Committees issued local bulletins. Wolverhampton's began on Wednesday, 5th May, and was published each day until the strike was called off.[174] The Communist Party also issued bulletins and newssheets. These were targeted by the authorities as quickly as possible, either by prosecutions for publishing 'false news' or for being likely to lead to a 'breach of the peace', or by confiscating their newsprint for use by the *British Gazette*. The daily and weekly newspapers also began to produce bulletins or shorter editions after the first few days of the strike. Most of these were against the strike and trade unions, and actively promoted the government's position. The overall result was that newspaper reporting quickly became dominated by those against the strike.'

---

173 *'Strike Bulletin', No. 1 and 2*, Sandwell, Archive, BS-KJ/8/3/5.

174 *Wolverhampton Trades and Labour Council Report*, Warwick, Modern Records Centre, MSS.292/252.62/5/52.

The biased tone in the reporting is highlighted by the West Bromwich Free Press on Friday, 7th May: 'An appeal has been made to all well-disposed people to volunteer help in the maintenance of the public services.' 'A large number of men and women of all classes have already registered, not of course as strike-breakers, but in the interests of the community generally.'. Also, many of its reports from outside the area show a close similarity to the reports in the *British Gazette*, the official government newspaper.[175] In its last edition during the strike, it published the following advice at the end of the sheet: 'If you see a crowd – DON'T JOIN IT. If you hear a rumour – DON'T BELIEVE IT! AND DON'T REPEAT IT!'[176] The *Dudley Herald* was similarly biased against the strike. In its editorial on Saturday, 15th May, it said that 'the strike is, happily, over', and that the 'response to the call for volunteer workers and special constables was magnificent'. Many showed a 'splendid willingness to carry on and … assist in the maintenance of order.'.[177] The tone of reporting and the words used also indicated an antipathy towards the strikers. A typical report was of a Dudley employer stopped by strikers on his way home one evening. When he 'thrashed the ring-leader' then took off his jacket and offered to take on all the others singly, 'they allowed him to continue'.[178]

The editorial in the *Dudley Herald* on 1st May reported that Charles Sitch, 'so frequently mild of speech and reasonable in argument', at a constituency meeting on Thursday night said, 'we like peace, but we are not going to have peace with

---

175 *'Strike Bulletin', No. 1 and 2*, Sandwell, Archive, BS-KJ/8/3/5:

176 *'Strike Bulletin', No. 1 and 2*, Sandwell, Archive, BS-KJ/8/3/5.

177 *Dudley Herald*, 15 May 1926.

178 *Dudley Herald*, 15 May 1926.

slavery. The essential condition of peace in industry is that the industry should give to the worker a right to a proper and full life.' The editorial responded that these statements are 'calculated ... to evoke applause' rather than 'a consideration of the position from a just perspective.' A week later, with the strikes now making an impact across the Black Country, and despite conflicting newspaper reports the editorial said that the 'response to the calls for volunteers was spontaneous' and the 'specials' were 'mobilised on Tuesday morning and almost to a man promptly responded to the call.'. 'Even on the first day of the strike' the editorial stated that it was clear that the strike was 'unpopular with the majority who were participating'. It quoted that a meeting of Dudley railwaymen requested their local leaders to do all they could to bring it to an 'early termination'. However, there was no mention of the almost 100% response of the men to the calls for strikes. In addition, the reporting gave little indication of the quantity of meetings and events that took place. In the week that Charles Sitch is reported as attending forty meetings, only five are recorded, and many of those are only described peremptorily.

With the announcement that the General Strike was ended, on Wednesday, 12th May, the *Express and Star* editorial called it 'the most welcome news of the past fortnight.' It called for the country to 'get back to work....repair the damage.... look for a just and peaceful settlement of the dispute in the coalfields.' The tone began to change the next day, when the editorial claimed that 'this was a victory for law. The dispute began with the breaking of contracts and therefore was illegal'. However, it called for both sides to 'forget all recriminations. Let employers act with generosity. Let workmen put their whole heart and mind into their work. We have to repair the damage of the strike, and that is the only way to do it.' However, this was very mild compared to the headlines on the front page of the *British Gazette* on the same day: 'Surrender Received By Premier In Downing Street'.

Photographs

Express & Star Bulletin: 4th May 1st Edition

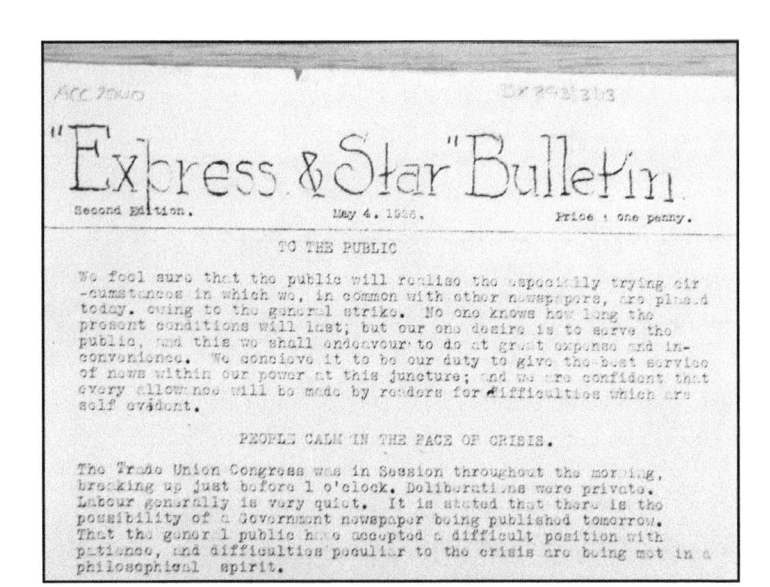

"Express & Star" Bulletin

Second Edition.   May 4. 1926.   Price : One penny.

TO THE PUBLIC

We feel sure that the public will realise the especially trying circumstances in which we, in common with other newspapers, are placed today, owing to the general strike. No one knows how long the present conditions will last; but our one desire is to serve the public, and this we shall endeavour to do at great expense and inconvenience. We conceive it to be our duty to give the best service of news within our power at this juncture; and we are confident that every allowance will be made by readers for difficulties which are self evident.

PEOPLE CALM IN THE FACE OF CRISIS.

The Trade Union Congress was in Session throughout the morning, breaking up just before 1 o'clock. Deliberations were private. Labour generally is very quiet. It is stated that there is the possibility of a Government newspaper being published tomorrow. That the general public have accepted a difficult position with patience, and difficulties peculiar to the crisis are being met in a philosophical spirit.

Express & Star Bulletin 4th May 2nd Edition

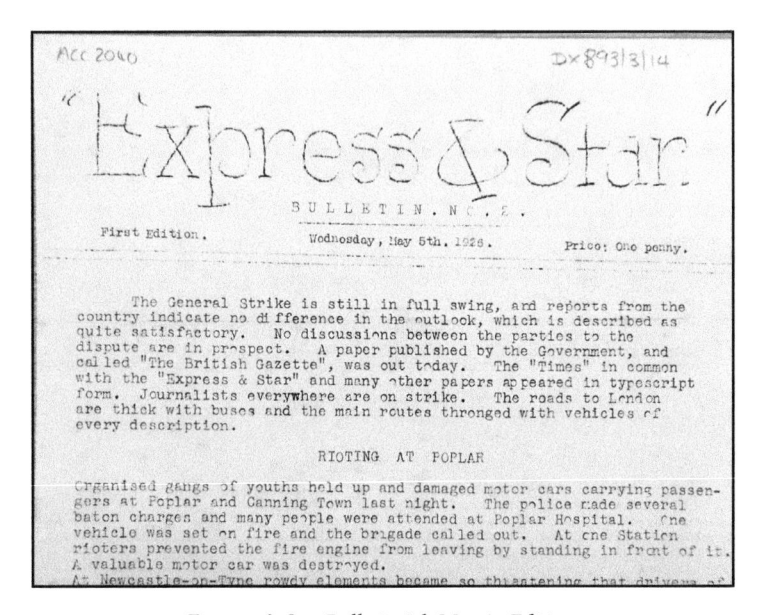

"Express & Star"

BULLETIN. No. 2.

First Edition.   Wednesday, May 5th. 1926.   Price: One penny.

The General Strike is still in full swing, and reports from the country indicate no difference in the outlook, which is described as quite satisfactory. No discussions between the parties to the dispute are in prospect. A paper published by the Government, and called "The British Gazette", was out today. The "Times" in common with the "Express & Star" and many other papers appeared in typescript form. Journalists everywhere are on strike. The roads to London are thick with buses and the main routes thronged with vehicles of every description.

RIOTING AT POPLAR

Organised gangs of youths held up and damaged motor cars carrying passengers at Poplar and Canning Town last night. The police made several baton charges and many people were attended at Poplar Hospital. One vehicle was set on fire and the brigade called out. At one Station rioters prevented the fire engine from leaving by standing in front of it. A valuable motor car was destroyed.

At Newcastle-on-Tyne rowdy elements became so threatening that drivers of

Express & Star Bulletin 5th May 1stEdition

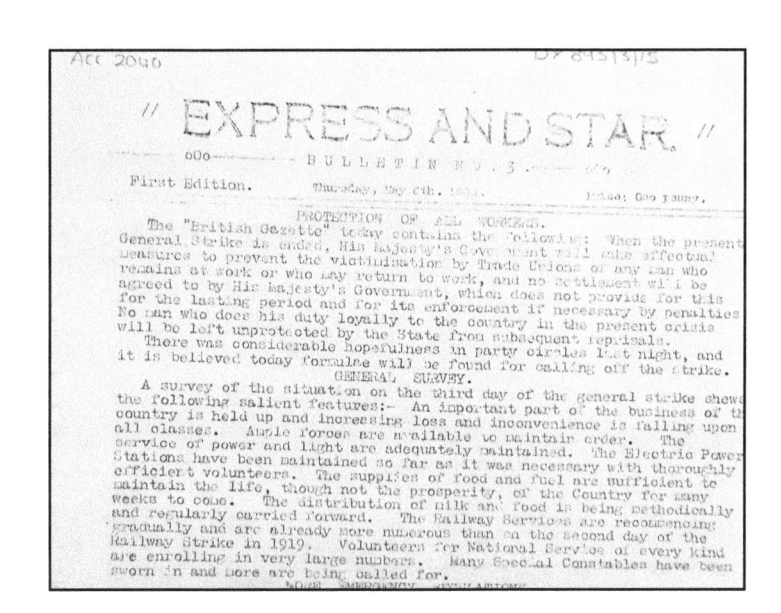

> Acc 2040
>
> ## "EXPRESS AND STAR."
> BULLETIN NO. 3
>
> First Edition.   Thursday, May 6th 1926.   Price: One Penny.
>
> PROTECTION OF ALL WORKERS.
> The "British Gazette" today contains the following: When the present General Strike is ended, His Majesty's Government will take effectual measures to prevent the victimisation by Trade Unions of any man who remains at work or who may return to work, and no settlement will be agreed to by His Majesty's Government, which does not provide for this for the lasting period and for its enforcement if necessary by penalties No man who does his duty loyally to the country in the present crisis will be left unprotected by the State from subsequent reprisals.
> There was considerable hopefulness in party circles last night, and it is believed today formulae will be found for calling off the strike.
> GENERAL SURVEY.
> A survey of the situation on the third day of the general strike shows the following salient features:- An important part of the business of the country is held up and increasing loss and inconvenience is falling upon all classes. Ample forces are available to maintain order. The service of power and light are adequately maintained. The Electric Power Stations have been maintained so far as it was necessary with thoroughly efficient volunteers. The supplies of food and fuel are sufficient to maintain the life, though not the prosperity, of the Country for many weeks to come. The distribution of milk and food is being methodically and regularly carried forward. The Railway Services are recommencing gradually and are already more numerous than on the second day of the Railway Strike in 1919. Volunteers for National Service of every kind are enrolling in very large numbers. Many Special Constables have been sworn in and more are being called for.

Express & Star Bulletin 6th May 1st Edition

Parkfield Colliery

Lift Please

Wolverhampton Thanksgiving Service

PEACE MOVES

BELIEVED TO BE IN PROGRESS BENEATH THE SURFACE.

"THE TIDE HAS TURNED"
—GOVERNMENT SPOKESMAN.

GENERAL TENDENCY OF STRIKERS TO DRIFT BACK.

"Wolverhampton Chronicle" Office, Tuesday evening.

Although no official confirmation can be obtained, there is reason to believe that peace moves are taking place beneath the surface, telegraphs the Press Association.

Mr. Ramsay Macdonald had an interview to-day with the Miners' Executive before meeting the General Council of the T.U.C. Mr. J. H. Thomas, after a visit to the Commons, returned hurriedly to the General Council, and Mr. Ernest Bevin also came back post-haste.

It was officially stated by the T.U.C. General Council that there was no development, and that there was no information regarding the rumoured intervention of Sir Herbert Samuel, the chairman of the Royal Commission. A member of the Miners' Executive who was at Eccleston-square said that nothing tangible or concrete had yet been placed before the Miners' Executive.

"Without being unduly optimistic, I think we may say that the tide has turned," said the Government's spokesman to-day. "There is a tendency all over the country for strikers to drift back to work." The very satisfactory railway situation, he said, was indicated by the fact that the number of trains run has risen from 849 on the first day to 5,503 on Monday.

JUDGE SAYS GENERAL STRIKE IS ILLEGAL.

Mr. Justice Astbury, in the Chancery Division to-day granted an injunction against certain branch officials of the Sailors' and Firemen's Union, and in giving judgment said that the so-called General Strike by the Trade Union Congress Committee was illegal and contrary to law, and those inciting or taking part in it were not protected by the Trades Disputes Act, 1906.

Wolverhampton to-day instituted a bus service with ten vehicles in charge of volunteer drivers. Big crowds in Queen-square greeted the passing buses with mingled cheers and hoots.

Following yesterday's ballot, well over 100 men have reported for duty at Guy Motors, Wolverhampton, and more are returning to-morrow.

Seventy-eight per cent. of the moulders at the Sunbeam Motor Works returned to work this morning. There are also a few men at work in every other department.

The ironworks of Messrs. Hingley and Sons, Ltd., Netherton, have become idle, 1,200 being affected.

WHAT THE MINERS WANT.

After this morning's sitting of the Miners' Federation Mr. Cook said—

Peace Moves 12th May

The Churches

The churches were as divided as the public over the question of whether the General Strike was an industrial confrontation or a challenge to the constitution, and what their response should be. The Primitive Methodists, who were generally clearly identified with the working class, could not agree whether it was a miners' strike or a lock-out.[179] Christian principles led many to side with the miners. However, the apparent 'declaration of war' by the T.U.C. on the rest of the community was viewed as an un-Christian act. This confusion created surprising outcomes. The Archbishop of Canterbury, Randall Davidson, in his call for conciliation, was perceived by many, from all sides, to be undermining the government's position and therefore supporting the miners, whilst the Catholic primate, Cardinal Bourne, clearly denounced the strike. This division was remarkable because of the strong establishment position of the Church of England and the substantial working class background of the Catholic church. Some took a conciliatory position, some argued for not taking a position at all, and others, with a more Christian Socialist influence, argued for unequivocal support for the miners. [180]

Perhaps Cyril Lloyd, Conservative MP for Dudley Borough, represented a typical standpoint of the churches, when speaking at an Industrial Sunday meeting on 25th April. He considered it a 'profound misfortune' that there had developed an 'estrangement between industry and religion'. 'The industrial system of to-day

---

179 Morris, pp 323-324.

180 Morris, pp 318-319.

had tended to make the separation deep and severe'. Referring to employers and employees, he noted that they were 'from their own standpoint, seeking to solve very much the same problems… working for the betterment of their industries and those engaged in them'. Therefore, he 'welcomed an occasion such as this' when they could meet together in 'friendly intercourse, untroubled, unhasty… to consider…the solution.'.[181]

The Bishop of Lichfield, speaking at an Industrial Sunday service organised by the Industrial Christian Fellowship, presented a conciliatory point of view when he said that 'the present dispute does not have a clear moral right on one side or the other'. He seemed to support the miners' position: 'the best paid miner deserved every penny he can get'. However, he placed himself on the government's side when he went on to say that 'it seems that the present emergency….demands sacrifice,' at least of a temporary nature, a clear call to accept a reduction in wages.[182] At the same time, taking what might be seen as a logical and conciliatory position could be interpreted as taking a side by those involved in the dispute. The call by the Archbishop of Canterbury for a negotiated settlement did not please the government. It was not printed in the *British Gazette* until the last day of the strike, and the BBC was pressured into cancelling its broadcast of the Archbishop's speech.[183]

Some of the causes of the confusion in the church are reflected in the sermon the Bishop of Lichfield gave on 2nd May at All Saints in Wolverhampton, when he asked 'what was the purpose of a General Strike?'. He then ran through what he perceived were possible purposes, 'to show sympathy for the miners' or to 'show

---

181 *Dudley Herald*, 1 May 1926.

182 *Dudley Herald*, 1 May 1926.

183 Symons, p 160. Morris, p 327.

the solidarity of labour' or was it 'a class war'. Then his telling question was posed, 'What were the objectives of the T.U.C.?'.[184] Others pointed out the inconsistency in the government's claim that the strike was an assault on the constitution. Dr Norwood of the City Temple in London, one of the most famous of London's Free Churches, said in his sermon 'there is no attack on the constitution. It is impossible to witness the remarkable order on both sides and believe that we are in the grip of reckless revolutionaries.'[185]

The desire to be seen to be strictly neutral was obviously uppermost in the mind of many. Mrs Crawford, the Lichfield diocesan president of the Mothers' Union, issued a message saying 'It is not for us to pray for or against the cause for every side…. But it is our duty to pray for reconciliation.'[186] Many churches united around the call for conciliation. St Peter's Church in Wolverhampton, Wolverhampton Free Church Council in Queen Street, Dudley Parish Church and Tipton Parish Church were four of the many that held an 'intercession service' every day at different times.[187] However, not all churchmen took a conciliatory position. The re-elected chairman of the Willenhall Council, John A. Harper, decided that the usual parade would be cancelled and a church service held instead in Willenhall's Wesleyan Chapel in Union Street, where all shades of opinion were represented. However, at the service, the Reverend W Percy Hutton did not continue with this neutrality. Referring to the General Strike, he said that a 'vigorous attack was being made upon the first principle of constitutional government'. He called

---

184 *Express and Star*, 3 May 1926.

185 Fyfe, 10 May 1926.

186 *Express and Star*, 10 May 1926.

187 *Express and Star*, 8 May 1926. *Dudley Herald*, 8 and 15 May 1926.

the strikes 'anarchy, tyranny, lawlessness, foolish, useless, anti-social and anti-Christian'.[188]

Whatever the stance taken by local churches, general support for the Archbishop's call was high.[189] The railwaymen of Bushbury in Wolverhampton, decided to 'march as a body to the church service on the morning of Sunday, 9th May'.[190] When the Bishop of Lichfield visited Bushbury Church for a massed meeting 'of an entirely unsectarian and non-political nature' on Monday, 10th May, he found it full, with standing room only. In his address, he praised the railwaymen for 'acting unselfishly, they will not gain from this dispute, they are merely supporting their comrades, the miners'. But, he noted, 'it was possible to do the right thing for the wrong motives'. He went on to discuss 'the difficult clash of loyalty to their union and loyalty to the nation as a whole'. He then finished with a request that they 'let Christ guide their decisions.'.[191] A little later, a worker at a meeting between Sidney Guy of Guy Motors and the strikers claimed that the Bishop of Lichfield supported the strike. This obviously caused some consternation to Sidney Guy, who telegrammed the bishop about it. The Bishop apparently explained about his sermon to the railway workers earlier that day.

---

[188] *Express and Star*, 10 May 1926.

[189] Morris, p 329.

[190] *Express and Star*, 8 May 1926.

[191] *Express and Star*, 10 May 1926.

The Poor Law Unions And Unemployment Benefit (the dole)

Confusion and conflict were also evident in the area of social welfare and support. Whilst it was clear that a striker was not entitled to either Poor Law Relief or the dole, the exact interpretation of the rules was not consistent. Mr Buckley, manager of the Wolverhampton Employment Exchange, reported that dole could be paid to men thrown out of work due to others in their factory or shop striking, subject to the Court of Referees. However, the Wednesbury Employment Exchange refused to pay employees from the Patent Shaft and Axletree Company because the firm was affected by a trade dispute.[192] The Ministry of Health sent a letter to the England and Wales Boards of Guardians, reminding them of their statutory duty to relieve destitution. They were not to take into account their view of the merits of a strike in dealing with applications made to them.

Once the strike was declared, the Poor Law Unions began to organise themselves. On Thursday, 6th May, there was a special meeting of the Dudley Union Board of Guardians to consider the steps to be taken to 'cope with the probable large demand for relief for the families of able-bodied men rendered destitute by the national stoppage'. Arrangements were made, based on the 'widespread distress of 1921'. Test work was suspended, applications would only be received on Mondays and Tuesdays, all activities would be centralised, relief was to be provided in kind, not in money, as a loan,

---

192 *Express and Star*, 14 May 1926.

and finally the Clerk was given permission to 'engage such staff as may be necessary to cope with the work'. Test work was work at no or nominal payment in return for the receipt of relief. It included work for the institution, such as digging an underground tank for 5,000 gallons of water for fire protection purposes. The May instructions continued after the General Strike. Presumably they were required due to the continuing miners' strike. On 14th July, it was decided to allow a cash payment of up to 5 shillings a week in replacement of an equivalent 'allowance in kind', so that the total assistance did not change. On 6th October, payment to 'men for whom work is available shall cease'. Then, on 24th November, the final May instructions were cancelled when test work was re-introduced and relief granted only to men prepared to do the test work, and all applicants had to attend the committee when their case was considered.[193]

Other Boards of Guardians made similar changes. The Walsall Board of Guardians decided to replace the benefit of 50% of the rent with a payment of a flat 4 shillings per week. This meant less administration for the union, and that applicants received the money within one week rather than having to wait until they had proved their rent cost. The Wolverhampton union established a special Emergency Committee. It decided that allowances should be paid to the families of strikers only if they were destitute, at the rate of a wife 4 shillings and groceries on scale 1; a wife and one child 5 shillings and six pence and groceries scale 2, and so on. Any income of the man up to ten shillings was to be considered as for his own needs, otherwise it was to be taken into account when calculating the relief to be paid. If unemployment benefit was being paid, then no other payment would be made, except where there was exceptional illness.

---

193 *Dudley Union General Committee Minutes : February 1923 to February 1930*, Dudley, Archive, GDU/2/1.

There was concern amongst the strikers and their wives that the Boards of Guardians would not allow any relief. At a meeting of strikers in West Bromwich on Tuesday, 4th May, one speaker said that 'if the Guardians did not give the women and children relief they should form up in a queue, march down to the Institution and demand admission'. The Guardians would not be able to accommodate them, and therefore would be forced to give them outdoor relief.[194] Certainly, Wolverhampton's main institute, based in Heath Town and one of the largest in the area, had beds for 1,292 people, but on 1st January, 1926 it reported that it had almost 900 occupants. Therefore, the speaker was right about the limited ability to cope with large numbers of claimants of indoor relief.[195]

There was concern about the effect of the General Strike on the poor law rates for each union. The Ministry of Health's advised rates were based on what was found reasonable in the 1921 emergency, with a reduction to reflect the fall in the cost of living.[196] If the husband was entitled to relief, then the rates were eighteen shillings for the man, five shillings for the wife and two shillings for each child. If he was not entitled to relief, the amounts suggested were twelve shillings for the wife and four shillings for each child. Individual Boards of Guardians made their own decisions, so for example the Dudley Board allowed, if the husband was on strike, ten shillings per week for the wife. For a wife and one child it was fourteen shillings and six pence. For two children it was eighteen shillings. It then increased in

---

194 *'Strike Bulletin', No. 1 and 2*, Sandwell, Archive, BS-KJ/8/3/5.

195 *Proof of evidence of James Curtis, Clerk and Solicitor to Board of Guardians*, Wolverhampton, Archive, C-WCA/1926/52.

196 *Newspaper bulletins….relating to the 1926 General Strike*, Sandwell, Archive, EPH/A/561.

regular increments depending upon the number of children. It would be paid half in cash and half in kind, for example food and clothes. The Ministry of Health noted that, as part of the relief in kind, communal meals were a very effective way of delivering food to the families. Finally, the individual Boards Of Guardians were advised that it was their decision whether relief was a loan to be repaid at a later date or an outright allowance.[197] These rates were not high, being designed to prevent destitution. However, if they were paid over a long period to many thousands, they would come to a substantial amount. West Bromwich Councillor Sutton argued that, even though 'there was no Union that could pay many weeks' benefit', he had confidence that relief would be given, because 'there was a law in England that said that no one should starve'.[198] John Greaves JP, Chairman of the Dudley Board of Guardians, reported at the start of the General Strike that he did not know how much they would spend because already numbers were increasing. However, they would do their duty to the people in want and would call on rate payers to find the money.[199]

Despite the statutory duty and the desire to support the destitute, there were concerns about the costs the unions might incur. In Walsall, this was raised as criticism of the expenses of the Poor Law Union. The Board pointed out that seventeen shillings and four pence of every £1 received went to the poor, which was deemed higher than most, and also, that the existing six Relieving Officers were not able to cope with the volume of requests. They had case-loads of between 200 and 614, whilst the Ministry of Health stated that the maximum number per officer should be 150.

---

197 *Birmingham Gazette Friday 7th May 1926,* Sandwell, Archive, EPH/A/561.

198 *West Bromwich Free Press : 'Strike Bulletin', No. 1 and 2,* Sandwell, Archive, BS-KJ/8/3/5.

199 *Dudley Herald,* 1 May 1926.

As it turned out, the situation was not as bad as first feared, mainly because the General Strike lasted less than two weeks. The table below of Wolverhampton's Board of Guardians' expenditure suggests that there was only a small increase in overall expenditure in the half year to 30th September, 1926, although there was a substantial change in how relief was provided. Out-relief reduced to £15,946, a fall of £4,471 from the same half-year in 1925. However, Provision for Special Works and Equipment and Relief to Unemployed together increased to £12,905, up by £6,086. The impact of the small overall increase appears to have been absorbed by Estimated Balances, in effect the reserves, which fell by £4,300 to £11,700 in the half-year.[200]

---

[200] *Wolverhampton Board of Guardians - copy minutes of meetings 1925 – 1927*, Wolverhampton, Archive, LS/L352/199.

£	Half-Years					
Date	30th Sep 1925	31st Mar 1926	30th Sep 1926	31st Mar 1927	30th Sep 1927	31st Mar 1928
Out-Relief	20,417	18,689	15,946		15,272	
Provision for Special Works and Equipment	1,457	2,751	5,158		1,681	
Relief to Unemployed	5,362	5,615	7,747		3,849	
Total Cost	79,311	80,396	80,703		74,417	
Estimated Balance		16,000	11,700	9,500		17,218

Information for the half-year to 31st March 1927 and 31st March 1928 is not available.

Policing And The Courts

Inevitably, police operations were not seen as 'neutral' by the trade unions leadership, but instead as part of the government's response of strike-breaking. They were effective in this due to increased intelligence, the concentrated use of force, with 'the baton-charge...the stock response to disorder', greater centralised control of operations and improved equipment.[201] As already mentioned, there were some complaints made by the Wolverhampton Trades and Labour Council Emergency Committee to the Mayor about the behaviour of the police, and that the phrase 'the crowd was dispersed' occurred several times in the newspapers reports. However, there were very few incidents reported in the Black Country, and on the whole, the crowds were easily managed by the police. On 11th May, the streets around Princess Street and Stafford Street in Wolverhampton became congested, as strikers 'greeted' the return of the last buses to the terminus at 8:00pm. The 'huge crowd' was moved along to Cleveland Road, where they were contained to the pavement. There the crowd 'remained an hour booing and ironically laughing at the specials'. The police then 'left to go back to their station' and a 'large part of the crowd followed them'. Some 'remained on the pavements of Prince's Square till a late hour', whilst 'the rest went home'.[202]

The recruitment of special constables was the responsibility of the local Chief Constable. In Wolverhampton, applications

---

201 McIlroy et al, p 250.

202 *Express and Star*, 11 May 1926.

were first received on Monday, 3rd May, and the recruitment process began that afternoon in the Sessions Court. Whilst only men were accepted as special constables, women offered to help by providing 'the loan of cars'.[203] By Tuesday, 4th May, 'hundreds' were enlisting in Wolverhampton, and on Saturday, 8th May they were paraded at Wolverhampton police headquarters. Even so, it would appear that it was thought more were needed, because an advert was placed in the *Express and Star* on 10th May. 'The Chief Constable of Wolverhampton is prepared to accept a limited number of men of good physique and good character as temporary constables to wear uniform and receive 10s per day.'. This was a particularly good rate of pay, compared to what might be received in poor relief. Other inducements were offered to encourage recruitment. They needed only to sign on for the 'present emergency', and were required only 'to give at least 4 hours duty per day', although 'preferably 8 hours' were wanted. Injured special constables were 'entitled to a pension or gratuity'. In case of death, 'his widow will be entitled to a pension or gratuity and his children to an allowance'. A report in the *Dudley Herald* clearly stated that the authorities did not have the numbers of men they really wanted. Councillor Robbins, who was the commandant of Tipton Special Constables, said he 'wanted three more men for each ward to bring the force up to its full standard'. The police did appear to be under-resourced, because they concentrated on locations of most concern, rather than attempting to cover the area in general. In the same edition it was reported that the police had instructions to only 'parade the main streets' of Old Hill to keep people moving.[204]

---

203 *Express and Star,* 3 May 1926.

204 *Dudley Herald,* 8 May 1926.

Nationally, policing was generally viewed as conciliatory at first, becoming more provocative and aggressive as the strike proceeded. Arrests were for four main categories: Irregular Picketing, Breaches of the Peace, Sedition and Publication of False News.[205] It would appear that, although the Emergency Powers Act was used to ban certain actions and activities, such as mass meetings, most arrests were for breaches of existing laws, which made it easier to prosecute in the courts and uphold convictions on appeal. Efforts were made to ensure the courts operated as usual, both to show that the authorities were in control of the situation and to quickly process those charged with an offence and make an example of them. This would explain why 'prisoners were brought to Old Hill Police Court on Wednesday by taxi'.[206]

In the Black Country, there were no reported cases of charges arising for irregular picketing, which might reflect the desire not to be 'disorderly' in their strikes and picketing. There were no charges arising from the publication of false news in the Black Country, although one of the twenty people charged in Birmingham for printing false news in the *British Worker* was Thomas George from Wednesbury. He was fined £5.[207]

The largest number of charges were for breaches of the peace, where six cases were reported in the newspapers. In Wolverhampton, there were four cases and one each in Dudley and Tipton. There was a heavy reliance on police witnesses in the courts and a general tone of prejudice against the accused. George Edward Brabazon was arrested

---

205 Christopher Farman, *The General Strike, May 1926* (London, Granada Publishing Ltd, 1972), p 277.

206 *Dudley Herald*, 8 May 1926.

207 *Summaries of information regarding the General Strike furnished by Chief Constables in England, Scotland and Wales*, Warwick, Modern Records Centre, SSL/3/6/6.

after Detective Constable Neal and Detective Sargeant Hitchings said they saw him throw a stone. He denied it, but the Stipendiary Magistrate, Bertram Grimley, said they were reliable witnesses, who were close enough to see and to make an arrest, and sentenced him to a month's hard labour. Thomas Henry Turner was overheard by Chief Inspector Crofts saying 'take his staff off him and hit him with it', referring to a policeman. He was fined £10 and remanded in prison until paid. Detective Constables Pendered and Grainger said they saw Richard John Griffiths obstruct a mounted special constable. Bertram Grimley, the magistrate, dismissed the defence with 'if he [Griffiths] was protecting women from the galloping horse, he would have expected other men to have intervened as well'. He was fined 40s with 10s special costs, and a 'blow he received on the head during the affray was taken to be punishment as well'. Finally, in Wolverhampton, Police Constables Harry Donald Griffiths and Bover said they saw Florence Lawrence throw a stone. She denied it and produced witnesses. Bertram Grimley, again, ignored her witnesses and sentenced her to 14 day's hard labour, but she appealed. This case was unusual because it was reported to Walter Citrine, the General Secretary of the T.U.C., following a request for information on victimisation.[208] At the subsequent appeal on 9th July, the verdict was upheld but the sentence was reduced to a fine of £6 plus costs. The recorder's comments are noteworthy in that the punishments were regarded as severe even by those in the court system. He said that the punishment of the magistrate was during the strike when 'things were in a serious condition, and prompt and severe action had to be taken.' However, as the 'General Strike was some distance away now', there should be some mitigation in the sentence.[209]

---

208 *Police v Mrs Lawrence Report*, Warwick, Modern Records Centre, MSS 292/252.62/8/6.

209 *Express and Star*, 9 July 1926.

There was one case in Dudley, which highlighted that it was not always clear who initiated the violence. Police Constables Spiers and Williams reported that Joseph Ball said 'come on, boys, let's have a go' and an 'offensive expression'. Constable Spiers responded with 'come on, boys: if he wants it, let him have it', then grabbed Ball, who kicked out. Other police officers arrested Ball, who was taken to the police station. On the way, Constable Spiers 'struck him slightly with his staff' due to his earlier 'violence in the Market Place'. A different version was given by Ball, essentially that he was standing some distance from the main activity on the street. He was found guilty of all charges and sentenced to one month's hard labour.[210]

There were two cases of sedition, both in Wolverhampton, which were much more clear cut. Albert Llewellyn Darke was seen in his RAF uniform at the May-day parade in Wolverhampton. Around his hat there was a red band and he wore various hammer and sickle badges. He also carried a placard saying 'don't shoot'. Later he was seen selling communist literature in the Market Place. Charged with bringing 'HM uniform into contempt', he was found to be wearing his uniform in a 'contemptuous manner' and was fined £6.[211] The second case was that of John James Forster, who, at the same May-day parade, was seen in St James's Square, wearing a khaki army uniform on which he had red sashes, and carrying a red flag in the procession. He was fined £1.[212]

Whilst there were very few incidents that ended up in the courts, it would appear that there were many occasions of 'altercations between strikers and those continuing to work', which

---

210 *Dudley Herald,* 15 May 1926.

211 *Express and Star,* 19 May 1926.

212 *Express and Star,* 13 May 1926.

lead to 'fisticuffs'.²¹³ Why there should have been very few arrests is not clear. Even at big events which became disordered, such as the Market Place in Dudley in the first week of the strike, when the crowd became 'ugly' and the police drew their truncheons, there was only one arrest. Perhaps the police were content to merely 'disperse' the crowd, and the crowd did not want a prolonged confrontation with the authorities, as requested in the many messages from the trade unions leaders. More typical was the large meeting of strikers on the George and Dragon land in Blackheath, when no trouble was reported.²¹⁴ Whatever the ultimate reasons, the Wolverhampton Mayor was able to make a statement that 'peace and good order have been maintained and a spirit of goodwill has been exhibited on all sides' and that whilst groups of men stood 'here and there…discussing the latest situation, [there is] no untoward incident of any kind.'²¹⁵ A note of caution was sounded when the Wolverhampton Chief Constable warned 'idle spectators to keep clear of the streets'.²¹⁶ He was wisely attempting to ensure that the possibility of trouble developing was minimised by reducing the numbers of people at a scene. His caution continued as the strike came to an end on 12th May. Whilst addressing a parade of mounted special constables, he stated that he 'might retain the services of the special constables for another two or three days'.²¹⁷

For the majority of the General Strike in the Black Country there were few occasions when large scale policing activities were

---

213 *Dudley Herald,* 8 May 1926.

214 *Dudley Herald,* 15 May 1926.

215 *Express and Star,* 8 May 1926.

216 **Express and Star,** 11 May 1926.

217 *Express and Star,* 13 May 1926.

required. The situation in Dudley, where 120 Special Constables enrolled, but only a minority were used, was not unusual.[218] The Chief Constables for Dudley and Walsall, along with 51 others, reported that communist influence or activity was 'negligible' in their area.[219] Local police action against communists amounted to prohibiting all meetings at which prominent communists were to speak, charging two people with bringing His Majesty's uniform into contempt, and charging one person for making a seditious speech.

---

218 *Dudley Herald*, 15 May 1926.

219 *Summaries of information regarding the General Strike furnished by Chief Constables in England, Scotland and Wales*, Warwick, Modern Records Centre, SSL/3/6/6.

The End Of The General Strike

The announcement that the General Strike was over reached Wolverhampton at about 1:15pm on 12th May. According to the *Express and Star,* the men were 'not sure what to do, they were waiting for instructions from their unions', which is not surprising because, according to the Wolverhampton Trades and Labour Council Emergency Committee, the announcement 'came as a shock because it looked as though it would last indefinitely'. They announced that 'workers were not to return to work until they received instructions from their branch officials'.[220] Some of these instructions came through very quickly and were enacted immediately. The tramways workers' local union delegates received a telegram from Transport Federation headquarters to resume work, which they did at 8:00pm that day.[221] Others took a little time and a special communication. Councillor J Mark, Secretary of the Wednesbury and Darlaston delegation of iron and steel workers, received a telegram from Arthur Pugh, chairman of the T.U.C. General Council, on Thursday, 13th May, saying the General Strike was declared off and to 'make arrangements for restarting work'.[222]

It was thought that the process of returning to work would take some time, due to the disorganisation caused by the General Strike and the continuing lack of coal, fuel and materials. The railways would take about a week: 'some day next week' was the usual prediction. Vane Morland, the Walsall tramways and buses

---

[220] *Wolverhampton Trades and Labour Council Report,* Warwick, Modern Records Centre, MSS.292/252.62/5/52.

[221] *Express and Star,* 12 May 1926.

[222] *Express and Star,* 13 May 1926.

manager, said it would take a week to settle back to normal service. In practice, the tramways and buses appeared to return to normal quickly. By the end of May 13th, most of the tramwaymen in Bilston had returned and the service was connected to Walsall, and all the Wolverhampton and District tramways and buses were 'running as normal'.[223] The railways did take about a week. The railway companies announced that they were prepared to 'deal with race horse traffic' from 21st May, and therefore horse racing could resume.[224]

This pattern of a quick return to work, if not to normality, was repeated across the region. By 14th May, a wide range of different businesses announced that they were nearly 'as normal'. The Star Engineering Company reported that 'all departments will be open on 17th May at 8:00am.' A J Stevens said, 'practically all men back at work'. Guy Motors reported that 'all men who presented themselves for work are employed, at present 600 out of 950'. John Perks and Sons of Monmore Green said 'all back at work'. Henry Meadows Ltd envisaged 'practically normal working on Monday 17th May'. E.C.C. stated 'men returning on Monday 17th May'. In Halesowen, the Coombe Wood Tube Works reported that it would 'resume on Monday, with all 3,000 employees expected to be back at work by Wednesday'.[225]

However, other businesses reported some disruption. Clyno Engineering reported 'lack of materials means that not all employees are re-instated'. Sunbeam Motor Company said 'all men have returned and working as normal. The electricity department informed them that they can only have 50% supply,

---

223 *Express and Star,* 12 and 13 May 1926.

224 *Express and Star,* 19 May 1926.

225 *Express and Star,* 15 May 1926.

they are working on how to adapt to this with the least effect on the men. Shortage of materials are affecting some departments'. Harper, Sons and Bean announced that their car shops would not re-start until after Whitsun-tide [24th May], but the foundry at Tipton would start on Monday, 17th May. The Chillington Tool Company reported 'all back except coal and transport difficulties'. The disruption to the railways, with wagons and other equipment in the wrong places, meant that they would not be able to deliver materials to businesses, or, in the case of Tarmac in Wolverhampton, distribute finished goods across the country, for some time.[226]

At the same time, other businesses reported that they were still at a standstill, the lack of fuel affecting some industries and areas more than others. T W Adshead Ltd had 'problems with transport. Will start as quickly as possible'. The ironworks in Brierley Hill were particularly badly hit, therefore it would be 'some time before there is a return of men to work'.[227] Businesses with integrated foundries and machining departments appeared to be able to re-start their machine departments, but not their foundries. N Hingley and Sons Ltd in Netherton, Wednesbury's Patent Shaft and Axletree Co Ltd, John Russel and Co Old Patent Tube Works, and Foster Bros Ltd all reported normal working in all departments except those which were large users of coal.[228] For some businesses, the situation became worse after the General Strike ended. Samuel Platt Ltd in Wednesbury was forced to shut down due to lack of fuel and materials at the end of the second week, despite being able to operate part time during the

---

226 *Express and Star,* 13 and 14 May 1926.

227 *Express and Star,* 13 May 1926.

228 *Express and Star,* 14 May 1926.

strike.[229] In reviewing all these reports it is difficult to believe that businesses in the same industry or location did not suffer similar problems, so that Sunbeam Motor Company's problems with electricity supply were not also experienced by A J Stevens. Perhaps there were real differences in the effect of electricity supplies, or the ability to deal with them. On the other hand, it may be that some businesses were more balanced in their reporting of their situations.

For the workers, the surprise at the ending of the General Strike turned to shock and confusion as the terms of the ending became apparent. Efforts were made by local trade union leaders and others to bring a positive out of the situation, and to reconcile the ambiguity that the General Strike was over but that the miners' strike continued. On Wednesday night, over 1,000 trade unionists gathered in Cradley to hear Samuel Edwards, JP and miner's agent, and Wilfred Wellock, Labour candidate for Stourbridge, speak. Samuel Edwards spoke about the 'solidarity' of the strike and the 'marvellous' behaviour of the strikers. He also noted that many workers looked well 'for the rest they had had'. He asked for trade unionists to remember that the miners' dispute was still on. He reiterated that their cause was a 'righteous' one and that they should be supported in 'maintaining their wages'.[230]

One of the concerns of the T.U.C. and the men was the possibility of employers 'victimising' strikers by changing contracts, reducing wages or statuses, or by not re-employing strikers. Stanley Baldwin issued a statement saying that 'I will not countenance any attempt on the part of any employer to use

---

229 *Express and Star,* 15 May 1926.

230 *Dudley Herald,* 15 May 1926.

this present occasion in any way to get reductions of wages or increase of hours.'[231] Despite his statement, at a national level, 'victimisation on the railways was wide spread'. Strikers were taken back on reduced grades and reduced hours, at least for some weeks after the strike. Others were sacked outright, especially if they held responsible posts. Others were 'humiliated, lectured and reproached' by 'the top bosses'. In general, Symons believes that there was a general worsening of conditions for workers, and that victimisation took place on a large scale.[232]

The Wolverhampton Trades and Labour Council Emergency Committee noted that the railway companies, Guy Motors, E.C.C. and Red Bus companies were 'requiring workers to sign documents which would take away their rights. Employers were seeking to undermine the negotiating powers of the unions.' On 13th May, none of the Wolverhampton railwaymen had 'so far been re-engaged'. They were told by management that they would only be re-engaged if they signed a declaration that 'You are hereby re-engaged on the understanding that you are not relieved of the consequences of having broken your contract of service with the company.' Mr Jones, the stationmaster of Wolverhampton's G.W.R. Low Level station, reported that about 80% of men had reported to duty, but as they refused to sign the agreement, they had not been re-engaged. The same was reported in Brierley Hill, Wednesbury and Dudley. The Dudley men claimed that the companies were seeking to impose a new condition that 'all men would start as recruits and their previous service would not count'. This meant a reduction in wages, as increments and experience payments

---

231 *Express and Star,* 14 May 1926.

232 Symons, pp 217-218.

would be forfeited. They met at The Crown Hotel, and agreed that they would stay out until all men were accepted back without victimisation.[233] In addition, railway management had been instructed to take men on only as necessary and to start only a 'certain number immediately'. At Wednesbury, when L.M.S. clerical staff presented themselves for work, 'they were interviewed singly by F York, the goods agent, and re-engaged as found necessary in accordance with official guidance'. All of this complicated the situation at the end of the General Strike, and angered the executives of the three railway unions, who 'called for the continuation of [their] strike due to the difficulties of re-instatement'.[234]

Midland Red buses issued a statement clarifying their position, that they would not 'negotiate with unions still parties to the illegal combination against the safety and welfare of the state.' Also they were only prepared to re-instate their 'old employees as and when positions can be found for them if they re-apply not later than Friday 14th May, on the following conditions (1) no changes to rates of pay and conditions of work (2) negotiations on changes to rates of pay and conditions of work will be direct with employees at each garage (3) employees are to give one week's notice of termination of their engagements, (4) the company can suspend or dismiss without notice or pay in lieu any employee for misconduct or neglect of duty'. Midland Red stated that, as far as they were concerned, 'the strike is still on'.[235]

For some of the employers the situation, as they saw it, was summed up by N Hingley and Sons' statement in response to

---

233 *Staffordshire And The General Strike*, Wolverhampton, Archive, LS/S3318.

234 *Express and Star*, 13 May 1926.

235 *Express and Star,* 13 May 1926.

'rumours' that they had 'locked out their employees'. In their view, 'the workers went on strike without giving 14 days' notice, as legally required'. Therefore, the employees had broken their contracts and in effect had finished their employment. Employers were therefore at liberty to re-employ men on whatever new terms could be negotiated. This was legally correct, but not in the spirit of the Prime Minister's statement referred to earlier. For the railway companies, a 'source at L.M.S. in Wolverhampton' said that it was 'not true that railwaymen being asked to take a cut in wages to be re-instated. Instead, as the contracts of the men had been broken by the men, the company was going to deal with its over-staffing problems by only taking back those men they needed, and they may have to do different roles.'.[236] The Sunbeam Motor Company said 'contracts have been rendered void, but no new conditions are intended to be imposed', and N Hingley and Sons Ltd, who had issued the statement clarifying their perception that contracts had been broken, reported that 'no conditions will be imposed'.[237] Other employers, such as Star Motors, Clyno Engineering, Turner Engineering, A J Stevens, and T W Adshead Ltd, reported that either there would be 'no changes to wages and conditions' or that 'no new conditions would be applied'. The management at Harper, Sons and Bean, more in the spirit of the Prime Minister's statement, said that 'sixteen A.E.U. members did strike', but 'let bygones be bygones'.

Whilst some sections of the populace were in shock or anger at the way the General Strike ended and at the actions of employers immediately following 12th May, there does not appear to have been great relief in others. The impression is of a generally

---

236 *Express and Star*, 13 May 1926. *Dudley Herald*, 15 May 1926.

237 *Express and Star*, 14 May 1926.

muted response across the region. Although there were 'pleased scenes in Wolverhampton and Dudley' with 'men and women clapping hands'[238], public displays of rejoicing appear to have been limited. Church services were quickly arranged, with one reported at Bushbury Parish Church on the following day. Their Service of Thanksgiving for relief from the industrial impasse included 'prayer for guidance in the settlement of the Mining problem and for the establishment of permanent peace and goodwill', so there was a recognition that the underlying causes of the General Strike remained unresolved. On the afternoon of Sunday, 16th May, a thanksgiving service was held in West Park. It was ecumenical, with the Reverend Leslie Chown (Free Church Council) and the rector Reverend Prebendary Stockley (Anglican) presiding. Representatives of the Police Force and special constables attended, along with a crowd of about 5,000. The service was opened by Frederick Willcock, the mayor of Wolverhampton. The Rev Prebendary Stockley said that this was not 'a service of thanksgiving for the victory of any man or party, but to thank God for peace'.[239] The Bishop of Lichfield continued with his theme that, when looked at, the actual dispute and the General Strike of the last fortnight was a disaster, 'yet bad motives could not fairly be ascribed to the majority of those who withdrew their labour'. Addressing the railwaymen specifically, he said that their 'motives were unselfish, although their policy was disastrously mistaken.'.

On the same day, at the Wolverhampton Market Place, a meeting was held by the Labour Party. It was opened by Mr Allport, Chairman of Wolverhampton Trades and Labour Council,

---

238 *Express and Star*, 12 May 1926.

239 *Express and Star*, 17 May 1926.

with the words 'Comrades of the great strike, we are met to offer thanks for the solidarity expressed by the working class.'. The crowd numbered over 300 at the start and increased slightly.[240]

---

240 *Express and Star*, 17 May 1926.

The Aftermath For The Unions

The trade union movement was substantially weakened by the General Strike. The differences remained between the trade unions leaders, especially between the miners and the other unions. Frank Hodges, secretary of the International Miners' Federation, said 'the T.U.C. could easily respond with comments upon the leadership of the miners which would be far from complimentary.' 'This disaster ... arises from the noticeable disposition in recent years to fly away from economic facts'.[241] It caused widespread bitterness and left the trade unions movement defeatist and on the defensive for most of the remaining inter-war period. There was less propensity to strike after 1926, but the Great Depression, which began in 1929, was probably a bigger influence in the 1930s.[242] It seriously financially weakened the unions, to the extent that their funds were 'practically exhausted'.[243]

The T.U.C. began a review of the General Strike and how the workers responded. They divided the strikers into three groups: (1) those who had been on long stoppages before, for example miners and dockers; (2) those who had experienced shorter strikes, for example railway workers; (3) those who had not previously taken part in a strike. They found that the strike was 'solid' in the first group. However, there were signs of a drift back to work in the other two groups. This seemed to be because they had little experience of prolonged striking;

---

241 *Dudley Herald,* 22 May 1926.

242 Morris, pp 276-277.

243 *Dudley Herald,* 22 May 1926.

that increasing amounts of transport reduced morale and determination; the government pledge to protect non-strikers and those returning to work encouraged a return; Sir John Simon's speech on the legality of the strike influenced some; and finally there was a lack of 'intimation of progress'.[244] These reasons, especially the final one, reflect the lack of an agreed, overall objective for the strike amongst the T.U.C. hierarchy and trade union leaders, and an unwillingness to pursue the strike with all means available.

This division and lack of resolute leadership was to compromise the perception of trade unions for many years to come, and was reflected in the feedback to the T.U.C. from the Black Country. Wednesbury Trades and Labour Council reported that 'the trouble has been since the termination' of the General Strike, because before the 12th the men were united.[245] The Walsall Strike Committee sent a message to the Miners' Union on 14th May, 1926, stating that they were 'dissatisfied with position' and that there were 'calls upon G.C. [the General Council of the TUC] to protect from victimisation all round.' The Oldbury Strike Committee, on 17th May, reported that 'general dissatisfaction exists, as the idea prevails that the T.U.C. has let the workers down by what appears to be tantamount to unconditional surrender. Confidence of the workers in the trade union and labour movement and in the leaders has had a very rude and severe shock.'[246]

There was consideration of a 'back to the unions campaign', but the Wolverhampton Trades and Labour Council Committee reported, on 20th May, that 'after considerable discussion' and

---

244 Farman, p 275.

245 Burns, appendix.

246 *Protests and Congratulations Received By the TUC on the ending of the strike*, Warwick, Modern Records Centre, MSS.292/252.62/3.

due to the 'unsatisfactory state of affairs of the last week' now was not the right time. The committee did ask for support, 'correspondence' that 'will give some little confidence and support to those who are anxious to carry the banner of trade unionism when the feeling ... is very bitter in the opposite direction'. They went on to say that 'if something is not done quickly the friends of the unions in this district will suffer very considerably'. Presumably they were referring to the victimisation that was widespread in some industries and companies. They ended their report by saying that employers were trying to 'undermine the negotiating powers of the unions'. The lack of options open to the trade unions was revealed by the Committee saying that a campaign should be started to 'strengthen Trade Unionism' and that efforts should be made to 'get all back into the Unions', the opposite of what they said at the beginning of their report, reflecting the confused state of the union members and grass roots organisation at this stage.[247]

This lack of clarity of what to do after the General Strike was expressed by Cyril Lloyd, Conservative MP for Dudley, in a speech where he asked trade unionists to 'put off until calmer days the question of whether it [the General Strike] was wise or worthwhile', and that they should not 'let any question of foolish leadership or misguided action shake your faith in Trade Unionism'. He recognised that mistakes had been made, 'the rules and methods by which strike action was started may be wrong, but your loyalty to the cause of your fellows is sound and right.'. Looking forward, he said that 'we must aim at better rules and leadership in the Unions.'[248]

---

247 *Wolverhampton Trades and Labour Council Report*, Warwick, Modern Records Centre, MSS.292/252.62/5/52.

248 *Dudley Herald*, 22 May 1926.

The Aftermath For Others

The effect on politics in the Black Country is very difficult to judge, and it may not be possible to draw much conclusion from the result in the 1929 election when Cyril Lloyd lost his Dudley seat. Being a Conservative, he was clearly on the government side during the strike, but he tried to maintain some balance, and distance himself from the aftermath of the strike, when he said he wanted to leave the details [of the negotiations] to those delegated to negotiate a settlement, but his view was that the public were of the opinion that the government was correct in its handling of the affair, and he hoped that it would be soon over.[249] However, Jim Simmons noted that 'public meetings, usually sparsely attended and tepid between elections, were now crowded and full of life.' This was due, he noted on the desire workers had 'to win back, by the use of the political weapon, the ground they had lost on the industrial battlefield.'[250]

The effect on workers could be wide spread and difficult to quantify. There is evidence that the strike had a long term effect on some industries and firms, reducing the wages of the employees. A small but telling example appeared from Stewarts and Lloyds Ltd, who ran Coombe Wood Tube Works. They had purchased over 18 acres of land in the nearby village of Hunnington on 1st August, 1925 to build houses for their employees and relieve the local housing shortage. The scheme never fully materialised, although 14 'cottages' were built on some of the land. The reasons

---

249 *Dudley Herald*, 8 May 1926.

250 Simmons, pp 72-82.

given were that 'the General Strike of 1926 and the consequent short-work seriously affected some of their workmen who had thought they would take up the scheme'. The remaining 17 acres of land was eventually sold on to developers on 16th July, 1935, incurring a loss on the land of almost £525, 18% of the original purchase price.[251]

The longer term effect on businesses is also difficult to discern. Sunbeam Motor Company seemed to be optimistic about the future in that it purchased land in 1926 and 1927 opposite its works in Wolverhampton and began to build what became known as the Elms Works. On the other hand, A J Stevens failed to declare a dividend in 1927 and began selling various parts of its diverse business. Sales began to decline, but this is seen more as being caused by changing markets, greater competition and better competitor designs, rather than an effect of the General Strike. The depression which came in 1929 hastened the decline, and the business was voluntary closed in 1931.[252]

---

251 *Correspondence re housing scheme for employees*, Dudley, Archive, D4/1/C4.

252 S J Mills, *A J S Of Wolverhampton* (Sutton Coldfield, self-published, 1994), p 83 and p 106.

Was It An Industrial Dispute?

In 1926, there was a series of important changes in the General Council of the T.U.C., which gave a different direction at the top of the organisation. The railwaymen's leader was now James Thomas, who was not a socialist and believed that, if there was a conflict with the government, the government ought to win.[253] Walter Citrine became acting, then full, T.U.C. General Secretary. His view was that 'the British trade union movement was deeply embedded in economic soil'. They had little desire for revolutionary change, seeing the T.U.C. as primarily a reforming organisation. The new chairman of the T.U.C. was Arthur Pugh, a right-winger in the trade union movement, who, in October 1925, succeeded Alonzo Swales, considered one of the most left-wing on the T.U.C. General Council.[254] These new people were 'far from happy' about Red Friday and did not want to be drawn into political disputes.[255] During the General Strike they were less concerned about winning and more concerned not to unleash forces over which they would have little or no control. Those controlling the unions were more conservative than the rank and file union members. In essence, the leaders of the trade unions did not have 'class solidarity', but instead they had more 'sectional interests', which prevented the trade unions from being the centre of 'revolutionary change'.[256] Even those trade union

---

253 Postgate, p 235.

254 Renshaw, p 5.

255 Quinlan, p 53. Davis, pp 159-161.

256 Davis, pp 155-157.

leaders who wanted to forcefully prosecute the strike were divided. The more moderate leaders, such as Bevin, thought that after they had won against the government they could then deal with the radical element within their movement.[257]

The result was a desire not to cause trouble on the streets. One of the first actions of the secretary of the T.U.C. Special Committee, J. Whiston, was to issue a circular asking members to do nothing to cause trouble, and not to be led astray in any way. He said that, as far as he was concerned, everything was to be done constitutionally and quietly, nothing to break the peace. Individual unions issued similar instructions. The N.U.R. represented the general approach, 'Allow no disorderly or subversive elements to interfere in any way. Maintain perfect order and have confidence in your own representatives.'[258] On the following day, the T.U.C. issued a further statement that included the request that 'violence and disorder must everywhere be avoided no matter what the excitement may be.'[259]

At a local level, Labour Party branches were keen to establish a distance between themselves and local Communists. The Wednesbury and Darlaston Labour Party publicly 'disavowed the Communist element' in the town.[260] Also, it appears that the majority of the men themselves viewed it as an industrial dispute rather than an attempt to make a revolutionary change to the country and the way it was governed. Actions were taken to ensure that the mines would be operable after the strike. In Rowley Regis, the mines had been badly effected by flooding

---

257 Symons, p 135.

258 *Express and Star*, 3 May 1926.

259 *Express and Star*, 4 May 1926.

260 *Express and Star*, 7 May 1926.

during the 1921 dispute, and so many had failed to re-open that employment in the industry had fallen from 2,500 men to 1,000 in five years. Therefore, whilst all miners in the area went on strike, the pit safety men continued to operate the pumps.[261] The lack of violence at large public meetings, especially those aimed at preventing strike-breaking, and the ease with which the police managed these events, suggests that the men closely followed their union leaders' calls for 'order'.

Some used language that could be interpreted as revolutionary in tone, but they were actually referring to the government's macro-economic strategy, rather than expressing a desire for a revolution. Alfred Short, at a meeting in Wednesbury spoke on how the £21m subsidy to the mine owners should have been used. Stanley Baldwin should have insisted on them reorganising the industry, pooling resources, developing new coal fields and improving efficiency, with the threat that if they would not do it 'we'll nationalise the industry'. As it was, they were given the money with no conditions.[262] Wilfred Wellock, Labour candidate for Stourbridge, at a public meeting in Halesowen, stated that the underlying cause of the strike was the 'dispute between capital and labour'. He then went on to explain that the 'first charge on industry shall be a living wage for those who produce the goods', but that he feared that following an attack on the wages of miners, there would be a 'general attack on the wages of the workers'.[263] This was a reasonable interpretation of the effect of moving on to a gold standard that was too high. To ensure industry remained competitive on the world market, the costs

---

261 *Express and Star*, 1 May 1926.

262 *Express and Star*, 1 May 1926.

263 *Dudley Herald*, 15 May 1926.

of production in Britain would have to be reduced, meaning primarily the cost of labour.[264]

---

264 K. O. Morgan, *Rebirth of a Nation: Wales 1880-1980* (Oxford, Oxford University Press, 1981), p 213.

Or The Start Of A Revolution?

Some individuals and organisations saw the General Strike as a purely political dispute, a challenge to the constitution, or the start of a revolution for freedom of labour. This perception of the General Strike was not confined to the left wing. Extreme right-wing organisations had a similar view of the General Strike. It was thought that some of the volunteers to the O.M.S had been involved with right-wing organisations such as the British Empire Union and the Economic League which had been set up by George Makgill during WW1.[265] Julian Symon's view is that the British Fascists effectively merged with the O.M.S. during 1926.[266] R. E. Ledbury, the Midland District Government Emergency Committee's Coal Officer, is identified by Mike Hughes as a member of the Economic League from at least 1925.[267] However, the left wing, led by the Communist Party of Great Britain, was the most obviously politically militant, and drew the most attention of the authorities. At a national level, the Communist Party of Great Britain set up the National Minority Movement, N.M.M., as a cover for their activities in trade unions at all levels, including the General Council of the T.U.C.. Established as part of the Comintern's Red International of Labour Unions, it appeared to be behind the election of the militant Arthur Cook as secretary to the Miners' Federation, and of Fred Bramley as General Secretary

---

265 Quinlan, p 44.

266 Symons, p 23.

267 Mike Hughes, *Spies At Work*, (Bradford, 1 In 12 Publications, 1995), http://www.1in12.com/publications/library/spies/app.htm#app5, [accessed 10th August 2017].

of the T.U.C. in 1923. Fred Bramley is attributed by some as masterminding the decisive action which resulted in Red Friday on 11th July 1925.[268] However, others have said that his death from illness in October 1925 suggests that his involvement was more limited.

Within the Labour Party, several MPs and parliamentary candidates positioned themselves at the radical end of the political spectrum. Charles Sitch, Labour MP for Kingswinford, speaking at the Rowley Labour Club, saw the looming General Strike 'as a test of loyalty….we shall find out those people who are disloyal to their class.' He went on to say that 'those amongst the workers who do not support the miners will go down in posterity as traitors to the class to which they belong'. He saw the 'attack' on the miners as the start of a process that would 'proceed to every industry.' Alfred Short, Labour MP for Wednesbury, said, at the same meeting, that workers 'were on the threshold of the greatest struggle….ever…. in their fight for emancipation from….tyranny and poverty'.[269] At the annual May Day rally in Rowley Regis, which has already been referred to, Fred Longden spoke about the O.M.S. as 'an insult to the working classes of the country'.[270] The rhetoric used at the Market Place meeting on 16th May, which has already been cited, suggests a 'class war' was in the minds of at least some on the Wolverhampton Trades and Labour Council Emergency Committee. Jim Simmons, prospective Labour candidate for Erdington, in Birmingham, recalled in his memoirs that 'Those of us engaged on Socialist propaganda did not have to preach the class war – it existed – the mine-owners and the employers

---

268 Davis, p 159.

269 *Express and Star,* 1 May 1926. *Dudley Herald,* 8 May 1926.

270 *Dudley Herald,* 8 May 1926.

generally, aided and abetted by the Tory Government and their legal minions, were waging it'[271] Dan Davies said that if the strike had lasted over the weekend, 'we would have entered another era of the struggle'. Further, he expressed the opinion that food should have been rationed, but it was not, and as a result the 'houses on Tettenhall Road' laid up their stores.[272]

However, motives and objectives might be complicated, or perhaps language and message might be altered to suit the occasion. Charles Sitch spoke at a meeting for Industrial Sunday, as previously mentioned, organised by a group called 'the Brotherhood' at Dudley Town Hall on 25th April, attended by a wide range of different interests from 'the church, the legal profession, the employers and the employees' as well as local and national government. He considered the Industrial Sunday's ideals 'magnificent' and none 'more worthy of support'. 'To bring men and women of all sections of the community together so that their influence might be used, in a Christian spirit, to solve some of the difficulties which beset industry and commerce'. He denounced a policy of 'mistrust and suspicion' between 'the two partners in industry'.[273] His industrial, rather than revolutionary, rhetoric came to the fore at other big meetings with very different audiences. In Brierley Hill, at the height of the General Strike, in front of between 5,000 and 6,000 men, he stated that they 'did not want to defeat the government, what they wanted to do was secure the withdrawal of the lockout notices [to the miners] and then they would withdraw the strike notices and get around the table

---

271 Simmons, pp 72-82.

272 *Express and Star,* 17 May 1926.

273 *Dudley Herald,* 1 May 1926.

to defend the miners there.'[274] The ambiguity of his messages did not escape contemporary notice. Major W Harcourt Webb at the Wordsley Women's Unionist Association meeting on Wednesday, 5th May referred to Charles Sitch's remarks at the Brotherhood about the need for unity and good feeling between employer and employee. 'They contrasted oddly with his statement at Rowley Regis and Kingswinford that every worker who did not stand by the miners would be a traitor to his class.'[275]

---

274 *Express and Star,* May 8 1926.

275 *Dudley Herald,* 8 May 1926.

Conclusion

For most people their perception of the General Strike of 1926 was subjective and depended upon their perspective. Henry Hamilton Fyfe, the left wing journalist and editor of the Daily Herald, saw it as an occasion when the trade union movement successfully organised itself for a conflict with the government. 'I suddenly realised...what a marvel the rapid growth of strike organisation has been. On the first day, Bevin said: "Now we've got to appoint generals." They were appointed, and they have risen to their jobs'.[276] George Stanley, the Government Commissioner for the Midlands area, writing to the Dudley Voluntary Service Committee, said 'I am writing to express my thanks for the admirable work which you have done during the recent emergency.' For him, this had been a real and substantial attack on the constitution.[277] These people perceived the General Strike as a threat and implemented the government's preparations with 'energy and gusto'.[278] These different perspectives meant that nearly everything about the General Strike had been disputed, even its name. It was not, and was never intended to be, a 'General Strike' as far as the trade union leaders were concerned. In the Black Country, some workers in some industries were called out. Some industries were partially shut down by the striking of selective key workers. But a wide range of different workers were deliberately not

---

276 Fyfe, 11 May 1926.

277 *Dudley Herald*, 22 May 1926.

278 Viscount Samuel, *Memoirs*, pp 188-9.

called out on strike by Bevin, Purcell and the T.U.C. Strike Committee.[279]

Objectively it is possible to see that the majority of trade union leaders and members in 1926 entered a situation that they really did not want, an ideologically motivated confrontation with the government. The major causes for this confrontation were the macro-economic policies of the government, the intransigence of the miners and the mine owners, and the government's concerns about the power of the trade unions. The government was able to promulgate successfully the message that the strike was a constitutional challenge and was illegal. They were aided in their strategy by the actions and words of many on the left-wing of the Labour Party and the trade unions. The moderate trade union leaders were unable to keep the message of the strike focused on the industrial and economic aspects of its causes.

This is clearly seen in the Black Country. It proceeded the way the trade union leaders wanted it to. A cessation of work without trouble. Many industries were closed or substantially affected without a major effect on the essentials of life for the majority of the population. The danger of control of the situation moving away from the moderate trade union leaders to a more radical element on the left-wing was highlighted by the speeches of some of the local and national figures in the area. Government propaganda, through the local newspapers, were able to give these speeches prominence and keep the focus on the illegality and revolutionary nature of the General Strike. At the same time the need for 'compromise' and a 'realistic attitude' by the miners was promoted, along with the notion of a 'drift back to work'.

---

279 Symons, pp 51-2.

In the end the General Strike in the Black Country, as at a national level, was a failure and the trade unions suffered a substantial defeat. The original dispute had not been resolved, the miners' strike continued until November. The government's preparations continued to be successfully implemented. Victimisation was widespread, especially on the railways and in specific businesses. New legislation reduced the freedom of action for trade unions and financing the strike financially weakened them as well. Disillusionment with trade unions was wide spread and clearly visible to all. So, whilst not prominent in the history of the General Strike, the Black Country is highly representative of the causes, actions and outcomes of the 1926 General Strike.

Appendix 1

The Midland District Government Emergency Committee Officers

Commissioner
Lieutenant-Colonel Hon George Frederick Stanley

Chief Assistant
W. P. Elias

Deputy Chief Assistant
A Broadly

Coal Officer
R E Ledbury

Finance Officer
O E B Bridgen

Food Officer
T Pritchett

Military Liaison Officers
Lieutenant-Colonel J A Bannerman DSO
Major W O Browne
Captain J M L Glover

Police Liaison Officer
C C H Moriarty

Postal Representative
J Scott

Railway Representatives
T H Shipley
J W Enser

Road Commissioner
F C Cook DSO

Canals
A J Butler

Biographical Notes

These notes are intended to give a brief description of the main individuals involved in the General Strike in the Black Country. The length of the entry is determined by two factors, the amount of information that has been discovered by the author and the importance of the individual to the events that took place. Some individuals are relatively obscure and therefore the opportunity has been taken to give them fuller exposure than others who are more easily researched. There have been some people for whom little or no biographical information has been uncovered, these people are reluctantly not included in this section.

R H Allport – Chairman of the Wolverhampton and District Trades and Labour Council Emergency Committee.

A local trade union and Labour Party member activist. By 1920 he was vice-president Wolverhampton and District Trades and Labour Council and became president in 1924. He became secretary of the Wolverhampton, Bilston and District T.U.C. from 1929 to 1941.

Alderman Charles Sidney Bache – West Bromwich Conservative Councillor

(Died 1954) Captain, JP, Solicitor and Company Director. Alderman of West Bromwich county borough council and mayor 1913-14. Member of a number of different Societies and Boards. Chairman of Conservatives and Unionist Association, West Bromwich.

Oliver Ridsdale Baldwin – Labour Candidate for Dudley

(1899-1958) eldest son of the Conservative and Unionist leader Stanley Baldwin. Oliver was a radical left Labour MP. He wanted to reduce the inequalities in society and to create a better society. He campaigned for the Dudley seat in 1924, losing by 885 votes to C. E. Lloyd. In 1929 he won the seat by 3,043 votes. He was fairly low-key in parliament, concentrating on his constituency. For example cleaning up the industrial landscape of Dudley. He lost the seat in the 1931 election by 9,154 votes to Sir P Goff, conservative.

Joe Bailey – West Bromwich Labour Councillor

Councillor Joe Bailey, West Bromwich County Borough Council

Emile Burns – Communist Writer and Activist for the T.U.C. and the Communist Party

(1889 – 1971) Bernard Emile Vivian Burns was born in St Kitts in the then British West Indies, the sixth child and the fifth son of James Burns, the Harbour Master and Treasurer of St Kitts and his wife Agnes. From a distinguished family, one of Burns' brothers was Sir Alan Cuthbert Maxwell Burns who became Permanent UK Representative on the United Nations Trusteeship Council from 1947 to 1956. Emile was involved with the St Pancras Strike Committee during the General Strike of 1926, following which he produced a major report on the work of the Trades Councils. He was a tireless worker for the Communist Party of Great Britain until the mid 1950s.

William John Brown – Speaker and Labour Candidate For Wolverhampton West

(1894 –1960) trade unionist and politician. Brown grew up in Margate in Kent and served as general secretary of the Civil Service Clerical Association from 1919 to 1942. He joined the Labour Party and stood for several seats before he was elected at the 1929 general election as a Labour MP for Wolverhampton West. In 1931, he resigned the Labour whip during the split in the Labour Party occasioned by MacDonald's creation of the National Government. He joined the New Party led by Oswald Mosley, however, on the following day he resigned from the New Party and sat as an independent.

Thomas Arthur Cottrell – Mayor of West Bromwich County Borough Council

Made Managing Director of Martin Dunn Ltd in 1926, a factor of glass and lead, oil colours and stained glass work for both ecclesiastic and domestic purposes. A member of West Bromwich County Borough Council since 1916, he was made an alderman and served as mayor from 1924 to 1926.

Rowland Egbert Ledbury – Midlands District Commissioner's Assistant For Coal Supplies

(Born 1878) President of the Birmingham and Midland Counties Coal Merchants' Association from 1925-1929. Presented with a cheque for 250 guineas and a grandfather clock by the coal owners and merchants for his services during the strike.

Cyril Edward Lloyd – Unionist MP for Dudley Borough

(1876 –1963) Conservative Member of Parliament between 1922 and 1929, and from 1941 to 1945. A member of the Lloyds banking family, he made his career in engineering being chairman of N. Hingley & Sons Ltd for over forty years from 1918. He also held a variety of other directorships and was active in the National Federation of Iron and Steel Manufacturers, becoming president in 1925. He was High Sheriff of Worcestershire in 1935.

Fred Longden – Speaker and Labour Party Candidate

(1886 –1952) Labour/Co-operative politician. Began work aged 13 in 1914 he was awarded a place at Ruskin College, Oxford. He also joined the Independent Labour Party and was elected to its National Council. In the First World War he became active in the Union of Democratic Control, and was arrested for making a speech appealing for immediate peace negotiations. In 1916 as a conscientious objector he was forcibly enlisted, and sentenced to two years imprisonment for disobeying an order. Stood for Labour or Labour/Co-op for Deritend in Birmingham in 1922, 1923 and 1924. In 1929 he won the seat, but lost it in 1931. He re-won the seat in 1945, when it was abolished in 1950 he won Small Heath, Birmingham, which he retained until his death in 1952 aged 58.

Walter Thomas Maybury – West Bromwich Local Union Organiser

Greengrocer in West Bromwich in 1933 gazette.

David Ebenezer Parry – Chairman of Walsall Emergency Committee.

Alderman of Walsall Borough Council and mayor 1925-1926. He was a mining engineer, a colliery manager and JP. He was president of National Association Of Colliery Managers 1924-25. Chairman of the Finance Committee for the West Midlands Joint Electricity Authority 1926-29. A staunch member of the Methodist Church, he was Circuit Steward for Walsall, 1915-32 and Bloxwich, 1932-33.

The Rt Hon Frederick Owen Roberts – Labour MP West Bromwich

(1876 –1941) Labour Party politician and trade unionist. He worked as a compositor and became active in the Typographical Association, serving on its executive council. He served on the Labour Party National Executive Committee for many years. He was elected at the 1918 general election for West Bromwich, defeating the sitting Conservative MP Viscount Lewisham. He became a Privy Councillor in 1924, when he was appointed as Minister of Pensions in Ramsay MacDonald's First Labour Government. He held the same post in the 1929–1931 Labour Government. He lost the seat in 1931, but was re-elected at the 1935 general election. He resigned his seat in 1941, and died later that year.

Alfred Short – Labour MP Wednesbury

(1882 –1938) trades unionist and Labour politician. Began his working life as an apprentice boiler-maker in Sheffield. He became active in trade union matters and local politics. He became Secretary of the Sheffield Branch of the Boiler-Makers' Society from 1911 to 1919, and served on Sheffield City Council from 1913 to 1919. He became Secretary of the National Union of Docks, Wharves and Shipping Staffs. In 1922 he was chairman of the Management Committee of the General Federation of Trade Unions. He was also called to the Bar from Gray's Inn in 1923. From 1931 to 1935 he worked for the Transport and General Workers' Union. He was elected an MP in 1918 for Wednesbury until 1931. Then he became MP for Doncaster in 1935 until 1938. He was Under-Secretary of State for the Home Department from 1929 to 1931.

Charles Henry Sitch – Labour MP For Kingswinford.

(1887- 1960). A trade unionist and politician. He won Kingswinford from the Conservatives on 14th December 1918, and held it until 1931, and was general secretary of the Chain Makers' and Strikers' Association. He left school at the age of thirteen to work in a grocer's shop, but, with financial support from the Chainmakers' and Strikers' Association, he went to Ruskin College, Oxford, where he studied economics and related subjects for two years. Back in Cradley Heath he played a leading part in union activity, particularly among the female outworkers in the chain trade. He campaigned for their inclusion in the 1909 Trade Boards Act, which provided for the establishment of minimum wages. He was among the first members of the Chain Trade Board which within four years, in addition to setting a minimum wage, raised piece-work rates by up to two-thirds. He became active in a wide range of trade union activities in the Black Country, in 1913 he was appointed assistant secretary of the Chainmakers' and Strikers' Association and from 1914 to 1918 he was president of the South Staffordshire and Worcestershire Federation of Trades Councils.

He was elected to the Rowley Regis urban district council as a Liberal in 1913 but switched to Labour in 1916, he won the safe Conservative seat of Kingswinford with a majority of 2,888 in 1918. He remained in parliament until 1931 but made little impression mainly because from the end of 1922 he had to devote most of his time to the affairs of the Chainmakers' and Strikers' Association following his appointment as general secretary. When he lost his seat in 1931 his salary as general secretary was only £2 per week. He supported himself by using the funds of the trade union. In 1933 he was charged and convicted for the fraudulent use of union funds and sentenced to 9 months' imprisonment.

Outside of work his main interest was amateur operatics, he was honorary secretary of the Cradley Heath, Old Hill and District Amateur Operatic Society for many years and was also a leading performer in its productions, often appearing with his wife, Mabel Jackson.

Lieutenant-Colonel Hon George Frederick Stanley MP – Midlands District Commissioner

(1872 – 1938) Son of the 16th Earl of Derby, he was Conservative MP for Willesden East from 1924 to 1929.

Wilfred Wellock – Speaker and Labour Party Candidate

(1879 –1972) A socialist Gandhian and Labour politician. He wanted to devote himself to the exposition of the application of Christian principles to social, economic and political life. He proposed a literal interpretation of the New Testament and felt that the theological superstructure smothered the real message of Jesus. He agreed with the Socialist criticism of Capitalism, but did not agree with the Socialist solutions, which he considered too materialistic. He was imprisoned as a conscientious objector in the First World War. He was an active member of both the No More War Movement and the Peace Pledge Union. He unsuccessfully contested the Stourbridge seat in 1923 and 1924. He was successful in the by-election in February 1927, and was re-elected in 1929. He was defeated in both the 1931 and 1935 general elections.

ELLEN CICELY WILKINSON – SPEAKER IN WOLVERHAMPTON

(1891 – 1947). Degree in history from Manchester University in 1913. Became involved in the broad labour movement, the Fabian Society, Marxism and pacifism, the National Union of Women's Suffrage Societies, national organiser of the Union of Shop, Distributive and Allied Workers, the Communist Party. In 1924 she joined the Labour party and won Middlesbrough East.

FREDERICK ALBERT WILLCOCK – MAYOR OF WOLVERHAMPTON

(1863 - 1939) Local politician and businessman. He became a Conservative councillor in 1904, representing St Mark's Ward. He became an alderman in 1926 and mayor for 1925 to 1927. An active councillor he was at different times chairman of the General Purposes, Parks and Baths, Watch and Wolverhampton and Staffordshire Assessment Committees. He had a wide range of interests, being a governor of Wolverhampton Grammar School; master of the Freemasons St Peter's and Wulfrun lodges; vice-chairman of Wolverhampton and District Permanent Building Society; a sidesman and people's warden at St Peter's Collegiate Church; and became a magistrate in 1927.

Robert Williams – Speaker and Labour Party Candidate for Wolverhampton East.

(1860 – 1938) Trade unionist who was at various times secretary to the National Transport Workers' Federation. Radically enthusiastic. He supported international socialism in Britain. In 1920 he joined the Communist Party and on the joint executive of the Triple Industrial Alliance. He was expelled by the Communist Party for supporting decisions against strikes to support the miners in 1921. Left union politics in 1925, but very influential through his journalism. By 1926 he was advocating policies of industrial reconciliation.

Bibliography

There are many books, articles and other sources that may be consulted to gain an overview of the 1926 General Strike or an in-depth knowledge of one aspect of it, and different authors bring their own personal biases to the story they unfold. This bibliography is intended to highlight the sources used in this book, and therefore to give an in-sight to the author's influences. It is not intended to be an exhaustive examination of the material available, nor is it a comment on the quality of the material used.

Primary Sources

Fyfe, Hamilton, *Behind The Scenes Of The Great Strike* (London, Whitefriars Press, 1926).

Viscount Samuel, *Memoirs* (London, The Cresset Press, 1945).

Simmons, Jim, *Soap-Box Evangelist* (Chichester, Janay Publishing Company, 1972).

Dudley Archives And Local History :
Correspondence re housing scheme for employees, D4/1/C4.

Dudley Union General Committee Minutes : February 1923 to February 1930, GDU/2/1.

Earl Of Dudley's Baggeridge Colliery Ltd Half Year Report 1926, DE/7/2/2/3.

BIBLIOGRAPHY

Sandwell Community History and Archives Service :

Birmingham Gazette Friday 7th May 1926, EPH/A/561.

Birmingham Post Saturday 8 May 1926, EPH/A/561.

Minutes of West Bromwich Council Meetings, CB-B/1/39.

Newspaper bulletins….relating to the 1926 General Strike, EPH/A/561.

'Strike Bulletin', No. 1 and 2, BS-KJ/8/3/5.

Warwick Modern Records Centre :

Burns, Emile, *The General Strike, May 1926: Trades Councils in action* (London, The Labour Research Department, 1926), MSS.15X/2/266/40.

Croft, Harold, *Descriptive Account Of A Tour During The General Strike 1926*, MSS.292/252.62/13/25.

Police v Mrs Lawrence Report, MSS 292/252.62/8/6.

Protests and Congratulations Received By the TUC on the ending of the strike, MSS.292/252.62/3.

Summaries of information regarding the General Strike furnished by Chief Constables in England, Scotland and Wales, SSL/3/6/6.

Wishart, Lawrence and Corbett, J., *Speaker notes, Birmingham Trades Council, 1866-1966*, 1966, MSS.202B/S/12.

Wolverhampton Trades and Labour Council Report, MSS.292/252.62/5/52.

Wolverhampton Archives :

Bilston Council minutes 3rd May 1926 Special Council Meeting, LS/LB352/3.

Labour Party Minutes, Wolverhampton, D/LAB/1/4.

Minute Book of the National Council Of Women April 1924 to December 1931, D-SO-8/3/2.

Minutes Of Meeting Of Wolverhampton Council, LS/L352.

NUR Wolverhampton Number 6 Branch Minute Book, D/LAB/1/13.

Proof of evidence of James Curtis, Clerk and Solicitor to Board of Guardians, C-WCA/1926/52.

Staffordshire And The General Strike, LS/S3318.

Wolverhampton Board of Guardians - copy minutes of meetings 1925 – 1927, LS/L352/199.

Newspapers

Dudley Herald

Express and Star (Wolverhampton)

Secondary Sources

Davis, Mary, *Comrade Or Brother?: A History of the British Labour Movement 1789-1951* (London: Pluto Press, 1993).

Farman, Christopher, *The General Strike, May 1926* (London, Granada Publishing Ltd, 1972).

Hughes, Mike, *Spies At Work*, (Bradford, 1 In 12 Publications, 1995), http://www.1in12.com/publications/library/spies/app.htm#app5.

Jones, G. W., *Borough Politics : A Study of the Wolverhampton Town Council 1888-1964* (London, MacMillan and Co, 1969)

Kenefick, William, 'The Fall of the Radical Left, c. 1920 to 1932', in *Red Scotland! The Rise and Fall of the Radical Left: c. 1872 to 1932*, ed. William Kenefick (Edinburgh: Edinburgh University Press, 2007).

Mason, Anthony, *The General Strike In The North East* (Hull: University Of Hull, 1970).

McIlroy, John, Campbell, Alan, Gildart, Keith, *Industrial Politics and the 1926 Mining Lockout: The Struggle for Dignity* (Cardiff, University Of Wales Press, 2004).

Mills, S. J., *A J S Of Wolverhampton* (Sutton Coldfield, self-published, 1994).

Morgan, K. O., *Rebirth of a Nation: Wales 1880-1980* (Oxford, Oxford University Press, 1981).

Morris, Margaret, *The British General Strike 1926* (London, Journeyman Press, 1980).

Postgate, Raymond, *The Life Of George Lansbury* (London, Longman, Green and Co, 1951).

Quinlan, Kevin, *The Secret War Between the Wars: MI5 in the 1920s and 1930s* (Woodbridge, Suffolk: Boydell Press, 2014).

Renshaw, Patrick, *The General Strike* (London: Eyre Methuen, 1975).

Sephton, Robert S., *Oxford And The General Strike 1926* (Oxford: Self Published, 1993).

Symons, Julian, *The General Strike : a historical portrait* (London, Cresset Press, 1957).

Wasserstein, Bernard, *Herbert Samuel: A Political Life* (Oxford, Clarendon Press, 1992).

WEB SITES

http://wolvestuc.org.uk/index.php/wbdtuc/our-history?showall=&start=5

Index

A

Archbishop of Canterbury *see* Davidson, Randall
Arnold, Alderman 13
Allen, S. T., Wolverhampton Borough Engineer 30
Allport, R. H. 17-18, 91, 111

B

Bailey, Joe 11, 57, 112
Baldwin, Oliver 33, 112
Ball, Joseph 81
Barnsby, George xi
Barrett, H. 17-18
Bell, Councillor 11
Bell, Harrison 22
Bourne, Cardinal 67
Brabazon, George Edward 79
Bramley, Fred 102-103
Brown, William John 42, 113
Bache, Charles Sidney, Alderman 11, 46, 111
Bantock, Albert Baldwin, Alderman 12
Buckley, Manager Wolverhampton Employment Exchange 71
Burns, Emile 112

C

Chown, Leslie, Reverend 91
Cook, Arthur 102
Cottrell, G. E. 14
Cottrell, Thomas Arthur 11, 13, 46-47, 113
Cox, Alderman 11
Crawford, Lichfield diocesan president of the Mothers' Union 69
Croft, Harold x
Crofts, Chief Inspector 80
Crooke, Victor 56
Crump, Councillor 14

D

Dale, Wolverhampton National Council of Women 39
Darke, Albert Llewellyn 81
Davidson, Randall 67-70
Davies, Dan 17, 19, 104
Dudley, Earl of 2, 29, 50, 54

E

Edwards, Samuel 87
Evans, R. J., Councillor 12, 17

125

F

Forster, John James 81

G

Garratt, Councillor 14
George, Thomas 79
Gill, Councillor 14
Glover, J. M. L., Captain 110
Grainger, Detective Constable 80
Grant, Councillor 14
Greaves, John, JP 74
Griffiths, Richard John 80
Grimley, Bertram 80
Guy, Sidney 35, 70

H

Hannon, Patrick 34
Harper, John A. 69
Hazel, Councillor 14
Hodges, Frank 93
Horrabin, James Francis 33
Hutton, W Percy, Reverend 69

J

Jackson, Mabel 117
James, C. J. 42
Jeffs, Alderman 12
Jenkin, Dockers' Trade Union Official 55
Jenks, Alderman 12

Jones, Stationmaster Wolverhampton GWR 88

K

Kenrick, Councillor 14
Kidson, William 55

L

Lawley, Councillor 14
Lawrence, Florence 80
Ledbury, Rowland Egbert 102, 109, 113
Lellow, Councillor 11
Lewisham, Viscount, Conservative MP 115
Lichfield, Bishop of 68, 70, 91
Lloyd, Cyril Edward 67, 95, 96, 112, 114
Longden, Fred 22, 103, 114

M

Mander, Alderman 12
Mark, J., Councillor 84
Maybury, Walter Thomas 47, 114
McManus, Arthur 48
Mercer, Councillor 14
Morland, Vane 84
Mosley, Oswald 42, 47, 113
Myatt, Alderman 12
Mynett, Councillor 14

INDEX

P

Parry, David Ebenezer 11, 37, 115
Postgate, Raymond 33
Poultney, Councillor 14
Pugh, Arthur 84, 98
Purcell, Albert 107

R

Robbins, Councillor 78
Roberts, Frederick Owen, Rt Hon 11, 115

S

Short, Alfred x, 22, 100, 103, 115
Silvers, Owen 27, 32
Simmons, Jim 19, 96, 103
Simon, John, Sir 94
Sitch, Charles Henry 20-22, 34, 58-59, 103-105, 116
Smith, Councillor 14
Stanley, George Frederick, Hon 8, 106, 109, 117
Stockley, Rev Prebendary 91
Swales, Alonzo 98

T

Tanfield, T. W. 11
Thomas, James 98
Tomlins, A. N. 39
Tucker, Chief Superintendent 47

Turley, Alderman 11
Turner, Thomas Henry 80

W

Webb, W Harcourt, Major 105
Webster, David 43
Wellock, Wilfred 22, 87, 100, 117
Wesson, F. C., Councillor 11
Wheatley, Councillor 14
Whiston, J. 99
Whiteley, William 32, 42
Wickes, Vincent 54
Wilkinson, Ellen Cicely x, 33, 42, 46, 118
Willcock, Frederick Albert 11-12, 91, 118
Williams, Robert 42, 47, 119
Williams, T., Councillor 52
Wills, Councillor 13-14
Wilson, Robert 32, 42, 46-47
Woodward, Councillor 14

Y

York, F. 89

BV - #0030 - 071218 - C0 - 216/140/9 - PB - 9781911175995